CHARISMATIC GIFTS
IN THE EARLY CHURCH

Ronald Kydd

BIP 90

HENDRICKSON PUBLISHERS, INC.
PEABODY, MASSACHUSETTS

ISBN 0-913573-09-4

To Roseanne

CONTENTS

Acknowledgments

I wish to acknowledge with gratitude the permission I received to republish material that originally appeared in different forms. This was granted by Scottish Academic Press Limited for the section on Novation which was published as "Novation's *De Trinitate*, 29: Evidence of the Charismatic?" in *The Scottish Journal of Theology*, (1977, 313-318 and by *Église et Théologie* for the section on Origen which appeared in that journal as "Origen and the Gifts of the Spirit," *Église et Théologie*, 13 (1982), 111-116.

Preface

The initial motivation for this study came from my own experience of the gifts of the Spirit. Shortly after I came into contact with Pentecostal worship, I began asking questions about what happened to the gifts of the Spirit after the New Testament period of the Church's history. I quickly discovered that there were few solid answers. As a result I was very happy to be able to pursue this subject as my topic for research in a Ph.D. program at the University of St. Andrews in Scotland. The work you have in your hands is a thorough revision of part of my doctoral thesis.

As I began my research, I realized that the fact that I was a Pentecostal could be both a help and a hindrance. On one hand, it could make me more sympathetic to charismatics of the past and by doing so help me to detect traces of the spiritual gifts that other scholars may have missed. On the other hand, it could make me see spiritual gifts when they were not there. I have tried very hard to compensate for my prejudices so that the value of the work would not suffer. You will have to judge how successful I have been.

I should say a word about the translations of the material from early Christian writings which appear in this study. If a particular passage was directly related to the topic, I always went to the best text of the original Latin or Greek that I could find. Once I had looked at the passage in the Greek or Latin, I checked existing translations against it. If I thought the meaning of the passage had been effectively conveyed in a translation, I used that. However, if it appeared to me that a better rendering was possible, I prepared a translation myself. The exception to this procedure was the way I handled the selections from *The Odes of Solomon*. For these I relied on the Harris-Mingana translation of the Syriac.

Thanks are due to a great many people who have been helpful and encouraging. I began my research under the late Prof. J. H. Baxter. When he retired, Prof. R. McL. Wilson consented to assume the supervision of my work. I appreciate the advice and criticism he gave me during work on the thesis.

The last two years of research and writing on the thesis were supported by Doctoral Fellowships from the Canada Council. I am very grateful to have received that help.

The typescript of the present work was done by Miss Joyce Bartos. I am thankful for her patience and skill.

I must say a word about the contribution which my wife, Roseanne, has made. Not only has she encouraged me to get on with the revision and writing, but she has also played an active role in the project. She has discussed the whole matter with me countless times and has read the entire manuscript, offering very perceptive criticism of my sometimes lumbering style. Out of gratitude, I am dedicating this to her.

INTRODUCTION

First century Christians were a dynamic group of people. They were radically committed to Christ, and they preached the Good News of His life, death, and resurrection with terrific zeal. Their vitality was remarkable. When we read the New Testament, we learn of miracles, acts of raw courage, and explosive evangelism. How do we explain this? Where did they get their drive? Closer probing gives a large part of the answer to these questions: these were people of the Spirit. They were certainly preoccupied with Christ, but they were very much alive to the presence of the Holy Spirit also.

They often found that Presence showing itself in dramatic, unusual ways. John says he was carried away "in the Spirit" (Rv 21:10); Paul pronounces judgment on an opponent of the Gospel through the Spirit (Acts 13:10 and 11), and believers spoke in tongues as they were filled with the Spirit (Acts 2:4). The Holy Spirit was among them, leading them to do some very surprising things. He was also at work quietly and inconspicuously helping Christians to spiritual maturity,[1] but He showed Himself in powerful action again and again. New Testament Christianity was charismatic. Times when the Holy Spirit broke in upon them with great force were common to these Christians.

There are many observations which support this. To begin with, the records show that Christians in virtually every major New Testament center knew something about the powerful moving of

1

the Spirit. This includes Jerusalem, Caesarea, probably Samaria, Antioch, Ephesus, Colossae, Thessalonica, Corinth, Rome, and the communities to which Hebrews was written. We know that in some of these places worship was very much alive in the Spirit, if 1 Cor 14:26-33 and Col 3:16 are any indication of what went on.

We do not have as much information as we might like about cities such as Athens, Lystra, and Derbe, to select several at random, but maybe the kind of people who took the Gospel to them should tell us something. Paul, Barnabas, and Silas were all known as prophets among their brethren,[2] a name they no doubt gained by speaking in obedience to the Spirit's urging. It is unlikely that this aspect of their ministries changed significantly when they moved into the Greek world. They were trying to bring these new converts into the fullness of Christianity, and the Holy Spirit was a very important part of that.

The question I want to raise is: what happened after this first period of the Church's life? In particular I want to address myself to the interval between the late first century and about A.D. 320. I draw the line there, because the Council of Nicaea was held in 325, and it serves as a kind of watershed in Church history. Steps were consciously taken there to tighten up things in the Church, in terms of both doctrine and practice. Did Christians continue to pulsate with the life of the Spirit throughout this period?

I think the answer may be found by focusing upon the "gifts of the Spirit," the *charismata,* as the Greek has it. These phenomena were recognizable among the contemporaries of Peter and Paul. Maybe they will be in the later time slot also. But first, what is a "spiritual gift?" We had better know what we are looking for before we try to find it.

In order to come up with the sought after definition, let us pause over the most important New Testament passage related to these matters: 1 Cor 12-14. We will try to develop a definition from what is given to us there and elsewhere in the Scriptures.

Basic to the understanding of a "spiritual gift" is the idea that it is an ability which is given to someone by God. He is its source. It is not at the disposal of a man, but rather it comes into play when God chooses.[3]

Secondly, we observe that spiritual gifts seem to be tailored to particular situations. The main thrust of Paul's teaching on this point is his insistence that the gifts are to build up the Christians among whom they appear. They really only find their meaning when they are carrying out this function within the Church. Primarily, they relate to situations existing at the moment when they appear, expressing God's will or showing His power in them. Maybe an illustration would be useful. Let us look at the gift of prophecy.

When we consider what is said about this gift in 1 Cor 12-14, we can make some specific observations. First, it is speech in the vernacular. It can be understood locally without translation or interpretation. This it shares with another gift, the interpretation of tongues. Second, it draws its inspiration from God. Third, it is addressed to people who are present, having significance for what they are experiencing. These last two characteristics of prophecy seem to be the norm for any of the spiritual gifts, the word of knowledge, giving money, healing or whatever. They all come from God, and they all relate to the situation that exists at the moment.

However, we must not become too rigid here. When we look at the Book of Acts, we see some things which depart somewhat from what I have suggested is the norm. For example, prophecy as it is spoken of in 1 Cor 12-14 does not appear to be predictive, and yet in Acts 11:28 the prophet, Agabus, made comments about the future, which apparently came true. Further, the information which one receives through the gifts of the word of wisdom and the word of knowledge mentioned in 1 Corinthians seems to be implanted directly in someone's mind by the Spirit, but in Acts 10:9-29, we find Peter learning something by means of a vision. I think what I have suggested as a norm is still valid, but it is obvious that we must remain flexible about these things.

And so what are we looking for when we are looking for spiritual gifts? We are looking for the kinds of things we see the Spirit doing in the New Testament. It should be noted in passing that the lists of spiritual gifts we are given in 1 Cor 12:8-10 and Rom 12:6-8 probably should not be regarded as definitive. When you compare them with each other and with material to be found in Acts and Hebrews, you discover too much imprecision and fluidity of thought to allow that. Even if they were exhaustive, we would have to acknowledge that some of the gifts will stand out more clearly than others; tongues, for example, more clearly than giving aid. We will try to catch them all, but we are likely to encounter the dramatic more often than the non-dramatic.

In this study, we will address ourselves to the whole body of Christian literature produced between about A.D. 90 and 320. On one hand, we will come across reports of the presence of spiritual gifts. On these occasions, we will have to weigh the historical value of what is said before we may admit them as evidence. On the other hand, we will find people talking about their spiritual experiences in terms which will remind us of the gifts of the Spirit, although these phenomena may not be explicitly mentioned. These passages will have to be interpreted carefully in order to determine how close what is being spoken of comes to the New Testament picture of the spiritual gifts. The closer the similarity, the better will be the grounds for assuming the presence of spiritual gifts. This illustrates our basic concern, which is to discover how particular New Testament experiences carried over into the period following.

It should also be mentioned that we will have to be careful in handling what appears to be evidence of the presence of spiritual gifts. The quality of this material is very uneven. Some of it is very good, but on the other hand, some is quite weak. We will keep this in mind as we proceed.

I suggest that what emerges from a study of the sources is the picture of a Church which is strongly charismatic up until A.D. 200. In the half century following this date, the importance of the spiritual gifts in the lives of Christian communities appears to decline significantly and attitudes towards them change. Following about A.D. 260, there is no more evidence of charismatic experience, at least up until A.D. 320, the end point of this study.[4] We will review the evidence chronologically, which is in keeping with the basic argument of the study.

1
FROM THE EMERGING CHURCH

Have you ever sown grass or planted a shrub? I had my first taste of "husbandry" after we moved into a new house a few years ago. Our yard was like everyone else's—a sea of mud—and it needed a lawn. I chose to remedy the situation by sowing grass seed, while some of our neighbors opted for a quicker solution: laying sod. The sowing of the seed was the beginning of an anxious few days for me. The newly-placed lawns in the yards across the street quickly became lush and green. Ours stayed black. Questions began to flood my mind: "Is it too wet? Is it too dry? Will it ever germinate?" The concern, anxiety, and suspense grew until the grass finally appeared.

I get much the same feelings when I ponder over the sources for the history of the Church for the period before A.D. 150.

Now the Church looms like a mighty colossus over Western society. It manifests its presence by its cathedrals and chapels, its publishing houses, its theological seminaries and Bible colleges, its globe-encircling missionary endeavors, and its television spectaculars. Much of society may be rejecting the message and the principles of Christianity, but it cannot reject "the Presence." It is just *there*. But things were not always thus.

From where we view history, we know that Christianity "took," and from God's perspective, that was always a sure thing, but back in the first century, that outcome was by no means obvious or certain to the average casual onlooker. Try looking at the history of the first century of the Church's life with the same frame of mind you use while reading a mystery novel *after* you have skipped ahead to the last chapter and found out "who done it."

With what looks like agonizing slowness, the Church struggled toward stability and permanence, although the people who were playing out the roles did not realize that this was what they were doing. Their tomorrows were just as uncertain and as ill-defined as ours are. With the passing of decades, the New Testament was recognized for what it was. Scripture and organization evolved; Christians began thinking carefully about what they believed; and all the while, evangelism kept sweeping people into the Church. Christian communities must have lived in a kind of continuous tension as they were faced daily with the need to react to, then integrate a steady stream of new people, new ideas, new sacred books, and new ways of worship. Suspense grips me as I block out what I know took place and watch the Church unfold. This suspense is heightened by the scarcity of information we have about this period. Often we can only probe gently in the darkness in hopes of touching something solid.

It is to the first part of this dramatic period that we turn in pursuit of light regarding spiritual gifts, and we find it shining from one document and one man.

The Didache

In 1873 the library of the Jerusalem monastery in Constantinople yielded a treasure that no one knew it contained: *The Teaching of the Twelve Apostles,* or the *Didache.* Since its publication ten years later by Philotheus Bryennius, its discoverer, it has been the subject of a host of scholarly investigations. People have focused on questions like the strata of material it contains and the revisions it has passed through, the place where it was written, and the date at which it appeared. While there has been nothing like oneness of mind among the scholars, I think some fairly concrete conclusions have been reached. We should probably assume that the *Didache* was written in Syria, which leads us into the heat and dust of the Middle East.[1] In terms of dating it, we are most likely on the best ground when we place it in the second half of the first century.[2] Of course this makes it a highly significant document, because it then takes on the status of an independent witness to what the Church, in places at least, was like during the time when the New Testament was still being written.

It is interesting to speculate about how widespread the conditions the *Didache* reflects were. Who received the counsel it gives? How far did its influence extend? We know that it was important in the Middle East, especially in Egypt in the fourth century, but can we assume that the circumstances to which it addresses itself existed that far away when it first appeared? There is probably no way that that question can be answered, but there is a clue which may suggest that it was relevant to a fairly large segment of the Palestinian Church.

To a large measure, the *Didache* focuses upon matters related to a class of wandering ministers. In the course of the discussion, we learn that these people were expected to keep on the move. If all of this was taking place in a relatively small area, the people who were travelling from place-to-place would soon have become well-known, and the suggestions the *Didache* offers to govern and test them would have been superfluous. Therefore, we should probably conclude that the *Didache* spoke to people in a fairly large geographical area.

The importance which the *Didache* has for this study rests upon what it has to say with regard to the people who ministered to the communities to which it was written. The New Testament Church in Antioch was marked by the gifts of the Spirit. In both Acts 13:1 and 2 and Acts 15:32, we discover that prophets were active in the Syrian capital, and the impression we gain from the *Didache* suggests that things had not changed much in that regard. There are two features of the Christian communities from which the *Didache* grew which are particularly interesting for us.

First, we focus upon the attitude which the *Didache* displays toward the prophet, and we note that there is a kind of ambivalence involved: they like him, and they do not. We find a positive view of prophecy in instructions following the prayers which are prescribed for use during the celebration of the Lord's Supper. Did. 10:7 says, "Allow the prophets to give thanks as much as they wish."[3] The author obviously thought that whatever prophetic messages were delivered would be beneficial to the Christians who would hear them. In view of this, prophets were not to have restrictions placed upon their giving thanks.

This attitude is revealed again a little later in the *Didache*. We read, "And you shall neither test nor judge any prophet who is speaking in the Spirit. For every sin will be forgiven, but this one will not be."[4] When a prophet spoke as a prophet, his message was not to be criticized. This exhortation reflects the esteem in which the prophetic message was held.

At the same time, the author of the *Didache* and the communities to which he wrote were not naive. They had learned that not everyone who said he was a prophet in fact was, and it seems that at the time when the *Didache* was written there was a large number of men, both inside and outside the Church, who were claiming this status.[5] A suspicion of prophets (and of wandering ministers in general) appeared, and it surfaces in Did. 11:8, "Not everyone who is speaking in the Spirit is a prophet."[6] This concern led the one who wrote the *Didache* to lay down tests by which false prophets could be separated from true ones.

The first test mentioned has to do with what the prophet teaches. Did. 11:1 and 2 state that the content of a man's message must conform to the instruction given in the previous part of the *Didache*. If it did, he was to be welcomed by the community. This test appears to apply both to prophets and to other travelling ministers.

The second test is directed specifically to prophets and is moral in nature. In Did. 11:8-12,[7] the author says that the true prophet may be distinguished from the false by observing the man's life-style. If he shows "the way of life the Lord requires," he is to be received as a true prophet. Enlarging upon this, he says that while speaking in the Spirit, a prophet must not order a meal to be prepared and then eat it. He must do what he teaches, and he must not ask for money or similar things unless it is for someone else. Once the prophet has passed these tests and is approved, his ministry is not to be judged.

There are also regulations which govern the length of the stay of wandering ministers, who come to visit communities. Did. 11:4 and 5 say that at the most he may stay two days. This seems to be aimed specifically at "apostles," that is, itinerant missionaries, because Did. 13:1 states that if a prophet wishes to settle in a community, he is to be supported.

From all of this, it is obvious that the Syrian Church was developing ways of protecting itself from false prophets.

The passages which we have looked at from the *Didache* illustrate the dilemma confronting the author and his contemporaries. They wanted prophetic messages in their churches, because they thought these were beneficial to them. However, they were also very conscious of the danger of being infiltrated by false prophets.

The second feature of the *Didache* which is of interest to us here has to do with the relationship between travelling and local ministers. While discussing the question of officeholders and "the old free men of the Spirit" in the Church of the second century in general, Hans von Campenhausen states that they were both there and then goes on to say:

> The coexistence of these various kinds of authority is not felt to be a problem. To start in every case from a supposed opposition between two separate blocs, the official and the charismatic, is a typical modern misunderstanding. Not only do office-holders possess the Spirit, but the spirituals for their part, to the extent that they rightly belong to the Church, derive the power of their teaching from the traditional apostolic truth.[8]

Von Campenhausen stresses that charismatics and officeholders could, did, and should work side-by-side.[9] The *Didache,* while coming from an earlier period, illustrates precisely the point which von Campenhausen is making.

> Therefore choose for yourselves bishops and deacons who are worthy of the Lord, men who are unassuming and not greedy, who are true and who have been approved. For they are performing the service of prophets and teachers for you. Therefore, do not despise them, for they are your honoured men, along with the prophets and teachers.[10]

The first thing which catches our attention in this passage from the *Didache* is the fact that the bishops and deacons, the elected officials, were apparently doing the same things as the wandering charismatics. They were "performing the service of prophets and teachers." It is a little difficult to decide exactly what this service was.

At first it appears that Did. 10:7 might provide a hint, because it seems to associate prophets with the Lord's Supper. Perhaps they led this ceremony. However, we really cannot say this, because the *Didache* does not explicitly show that the Church of that time and place had assigned this responsibility and privilege to any particular group. If we cannot hold onto that idea, the only activity which we can be sure the prophets engaged in was the delivery of free, inspired messages and instruction in doctrine. Granting all of this, we are left with the conclusion that, in addition to any administrative responsibilities they might have had, the bishops and deacons were also teaching and delivering prophetic messages. This highlights a tendency which gained momentum as the Church developed.

As far as we can tell, in most New Testament churches there was a great deal of openness to ministry "in the Spirit." Col 3:16 is instructive:

> Let the word of Christ dwell in you richly, as you teach and admonish one another in all wisdom, and as you sing psalms and hymns and spiritual songs with thankfulness in your hearts to God.

1 Cor 14:26 adds, "When you come together, each one has a hymn, a lesson, a revelation, a tongue, or an interpretation." When they gathered, all believers were potential ministers.

However, even while these conditions existed, a different model was emerging: some of the spiritual gifts became associated with particular individuals. As I mentioned earlier,[11] Paul, Barnabas, and Silas were all known as "prophets," and the same thing may be said about Agabus (Acts 21:10). In addition to this, perhaps the impression we should receive from 1 Cor 14:28 is that specific people were being recognized as "interpreters," who would handle utterances in tongues. So, in the midst of a setting in which free congregational participation in worship was being encouraged, certain people were standing out as those from whom charismatic ministry could be expected. Certainly some of these people, like Paul, Barnabas, and Silas, had special positions of leadership within the Church, but there is no clear indication that Agabus did, and the "interpreter(s)" are not even named. This suggests that being in a position of leadership was not a prerequisite in order to enjoy an advanced ministry through the gifts of the Spirit.

Did. 15:1 and 2 carry this whole discussion a step further. There, as we saw above, the elected officers were also expected to minister charismatically. There seems to be movement here toward placing the responsibility for all types of ministry, administrative and charismatic, in the hands of known and approved men, who had been elected to leadership in the churches.

We should pause over another observation drawn from this passage in the *Didache*. It is worth underlining that both types of leadership, the charismatic and the elected, existed in these communities. It is true that the tone of the passage indicates that the wandering ministers still hold precedence in popular opinion. The author feels he has to elevate the bishops and deacons by saying, "Do not despise them, for they are your honoured men,

along with the prophets and teachers." However, the "organization men" seem to be coming on. The author stresses that they are
to be held in honor, not beyond that given to the prophets and
teachers, though, but equal to it. He is encouraging a balance
between the two styles of leadership, and he is doing so rather well.

The *Didache* has a lot to say about the gifts of the Spirit. While
the cautious attitude must be acknowledged and the rise of elected
officials noted, prophecy is still highly valued, and the charismatics
are active. The Syrian communities to which the *Didache* was
written sometime between A.D. 50 and 100 were very much aware of
the ministry of spiritual gifts, and they were not alone.

Clement of Rome

From a somewhat distant eastern province, our focus shifts to
the heart of the Roman Empire itself, the "Eternal City." Our
attention is caught by Clement, who is traditionally regarded to be
the third bishop of Rome. Late in the first century of our era[12] on
behalf of the Roman church, he addressed a letter to the Christian
community in Corinth. Difficulties had arisen there, and he was
trying to restore order.

Embedded in this passionate appeal for understanding and coop-
eration is a passage which makes Clement of importance to this
study—"So let our whole body be preserved in Christ Jesus . . . ,
and let each put himself at the service of his neighbour as his
particular spiritual gift dictates."[13]

Our discussion will revolve around the expression "spiritual
gift." (A form of *charisma* is used in the original.) The basic
question relates to the interpretation of this expression here,
bearing in mind the meaning it carries in Rom 12:6 and 1 Cor 12:4.
In those passages it refers to unusual abilities which God gives to
people to help them minister to others. Is that what it means here?
If so, this passage provides us with evidence that the spiritual gifts
were in operation among Roman Christians toward the end of the
first century. I think there are a couple of considerations which
suggest that this is what we have before us.

First, we note the context within which the expression appears.
Clement is talking about how Christians should behave in the
Church. In 1 Clem. 37:5-38:1a, he illustrates his point by drawing a
comparison between the Church and the human body. "The
head," he says, "is nothing without the feet, just as the feet are
nothing without the head." As parts of the body cannot function in

isolation from each other, so the effectiveness of a church is shattered when its members are not pulling together. Clement is building a case for unity and mutual concern, and he places the spiritual gifts right in the middle of it. He thinks they are important in helping Christians to function as a body.

This is exactly the same backdrop against which Paul places his discussions of the gifts of the Spirit. The key passages in Paul's treatment of the gifts are found in Romans 12 and 1 Corinthians 12. In Romans, the comparison of the Church with a body immediately precedes what Paul says about spiritual gifts (Rom 12:4 and 5). A rather lengthy passage (1 Cor 12:12-26) is devoted to the comparison in 1 Corinthians, and it appears right in the midst of the extended treatment being given to the gifts of the Spirit.

Secondly, we turn attention to the function of spiritual gifts. The passage from Clement's work which we are considering reveals his thinking rather clearly. They show each Christian what he should do to put himself at the disposal of others. The gifts find their meaning in ministry. They are given as means of blessing to others.

Paul has precisely the same focus. The fact that the purpose of the gifts is fulfilled only in service to others is implicit in Rom 12:6-8, and this is explicitly stated in the Corinthian correspondence. 1 Cor 12:7 says they are given for "the common good," while 14:4,5, and 26 emphasize the "edification" of the group in which the gifts are manifested. There is no doubt in Paul's mind but that the thrust of spiritual ministry is outward toward others.

These similarities between the thinking of Paul and Clement about the spiritual gifts are significant. The fact that they share a common understanding about the function of the gifts and that what they say about them appears in very similar literary contexts suggests that they are talking about the same things. "Spiritual gifts" to Clement probably means the same thing as it does to Paul, and Clement says that they are to have an important role in the help which Christians extend to others. This looks like evidence that the gifts of the Spirit were to be found among the Christians at Rome toward the end of the first century. `

The first century was an exceptionally dramatic period in the life of the Church. Christians were forced to cope with the influx of new people, with the need to organize, with evaluation of books claiming to be Scripture, and with misunderstanding in the society around them. They did not handle this situation without concern, but they did handle it.

We are able to gain impressions about their thinking and their experiences of the Christian faith not only through the New Testament books but also from a reading of the *Didache* and Clement's letter to the Corinthians. The early Christians, as we see them in the New Testament, were very much open to the ministry of the Spirit. Many, many of them must have been charismatics in the fullest sense of that word. The Christians whom we see in the other two documents differ very little in this regard. These sources add their information to what we can draw from the New Testament, leading us to the conclusion that the spiritual gifts were important features of Christian experience throughout the first century. How does this carry over into the next century?

2

FROM THE SHADOWS

When we move into the first half of the second century A.D., the darkness hanging over the history of the Christian Church deepens. As we try to penetrate first century Christianity, we can resort to the twenty-seven books of the New Testament, the *Didache*, Clement's letter, and then to other deposits of information, such as archaeology and the study of inscriptions. The inscriptions and archaeology remain at our disposal as we pass the century mark, but the number of written sources to which we can refer falls off drastically.

And yet, we know that there must have been a great deal of activity going on among Christians during this period. There is no doubt that the Church continued to grow dramatically. Christians continued to be evangelists. However, for the most part we are simply left guessing as to what actually happened. What this does mean, of course, is that the written material which has survived from this period is of immense value.

As we focus upon the religious experience of Christians in the early second century, and in particular upon the gifts of the Spirit, we discover that a warm sense of God's presence persisted and that the gifts were still present. Evidence may be mined from two sources.

Ignatius of Antioch

We address ourselves first of all to material coming from

Ignatius of Antioch. This man stands out as one of the earliest bishops in the history of the Church, and he lives for us through seven letters which he wrote sometime between A.D. 98 and 117, while on his way to martyrdom in Rome.[1] These documents have received a great deal of scholarly attention. They have been subjected to examination in minute detail from a bewildering array of angles in order to capitalize on every scrap of information about the Early Church that they contain. It makes me stop and wonder how this condemned and harassed man would have reacted if he could have known the intensity of the curiosity with which his hurriedly dashed-off notes would some day be scrutinized. Of course he did not know, and he was able to write with a freedom and a frankness which reveals much about himself and the situation he was living in. The place of importance which has been granted to Ignatius' letters is by no means inappropriate.

Studies of Ignatius have examined many different questions: what did he think about the Church? what kind of ministerial setup did he promote? what heresies did he struggle with? and so on. However, there is one facet of the man which frequently escapes serious treatment in these studies. Ignatius was a Christian prophet with a high regard for the gifts of the Spirit. First we will look at passages from his letters which demonstrate this, and then we will think about the implications.

The first passage we will consider is drawn from a letter Ignatius wrote to another bishop, Polycarp of Smyrna, famous in his own right as a Christian martyr. We see Ignatius encouraging Polycarp to "ask for invisible things so that they may be made manifest to you in order that you may lack nothing and abound with all spiritual gifts."[2]

There are a couple of things we should notice about this piece of advice. First, Polycarp is encouraged to ask (God, most likely) for the privilege of seeing invisible things. It may be strange to our ears to hear one bishop urge another to pray for revelations, but that seems to be what is happening.

Secondly, Ignatius offers this advice for an interesting reason. He does not want Polycarp to be deficient in any way, but, rather, he wants him to have all kinds of spiritual gifts. The word used is again a form of *charisma,* and it seems to be used in the same sense as Paul gives it in Rom 12:6 and 1 Cor 12:4. In fact, Ignatius sounds very much like the Apostle, whom we hear exhorting the Corinthians, "Earnestly desire the spiritual gifts, especially that you may prophesy" (1 Cor 14:1). He does not tell Polycarp to seek any particular gift, but, rather, urges him to live a generally gift-filled life. He seems to want his friend to be prepared to exercise whatever gift God might want to use in a given situation. Ignatius emerges from this passage as a man with a lot of respect for the gifts of the Spirit.

The second passage to which we will give attention goes even further in establishing Ignatius' position as a prophet. He says:

> While I was among you, I cried out, I was speaking with a loud voice, God's voice, "Pay attention to the bishop, to the presbytery and deacons." And some were suspecting that I said these things as one who had had prior information about a division which certain people had caused, but he for whom I am in bonds is my witness that I did not get this information from any man. But the Spirit proclaimed aloud, saying, "Do nothing without the bishop; keep your flesh as the temple of God; love unity; flee divisions; be imitators of Jesus Christ as he is of his Father."[3]

There are two features of this quotation which indicate that Ignatius thought he was speaking prophetically on this occasion. First, note what he says before giving a brief summary of his message, "I was speaking with a loud voice, God's voice." During the time when Ignatius lived, using a very loud voice when speaking in a religious context was regarded by both Christians and non-Christians alike as a hallmark of a prophet. When you spoke under the control of some god or other, you did so at the top of your lungs! Therefore, when Ignatius points out that he spoke with a loud voice, he is not adding a trivial detail, he was really claiming to have been under God's control.

Secondly, how did he respond when his message was challenged? What he said was so accurate that suspicions were aroused about its origin: some thought the visiting bishop had been carefully briefed. This he flatly denied, insisting that it had not been he who had spoken but the Spirit. As far as he was concerned, he was a prophet.

F. A. Schilling saw this aspect of Ignatius very clearly and placed a great deal of emphasis upon it. He cited several passages in which Ignatius speaks of revelations which he had received (Rom. 7:2; Eph. 20:2; Trall. 5, and the one which we have been talking about, Phld. 7) and then said, "From these self-revelations we know that Ignatius firmly considered himself a prophet, though he did not call himself one."[4]

Assuming, then, that Ignatius did minister as a prophet and did think highly of spiritual gifts, what significance does this have for the history of the Early Church in general and for our study of the gifts of the Spirit in particular? In answering this question, it is important that we remember that Ignatius' letters provide material which is relevant to a fairly large geographical area. First and foremost of course, he is a witness to Syrian, and more specifically, to Antiochene Christianity. The circumstances in which he wrote would have made it very difficult for him to adopt different ideas about how Christians should do things or to develop a new theological system. He probably came across some new ideas as he travelled through Asia Minor, but it is very unlikely that his own thinking underwent any major changes. He was not a visiting scholar on a lecture tour. The peace in which he could think and write hung upon the whim of the callous soldiers who were escorting him to his death and upon the needs of the brethren who sought him out. He must have had very little time to himself. The ideas which we find expressed in his letters would be those which he had hammered out during his active life in Antioch before his arrest.

However, Ignatius also throws a great deal of light upon Christianity as it was found in Asia Minor in the early second century. The only writings of his in existence, which may well be the sum total of his output, are seven letters which were written to churches and people in Asia Minor from two cities in Asia Minor, Smyrna and Troas. These letters deal with situations existing among Christians in these cities, and they are, therefore, invaluable sources of information about Christianity of the day in that region.

With that behind us, I would like to suggest that the fact that Ignatius was a prophet-bishop is historically significant in at least two ways. First, it points toward the conclusion that Christians in both Syria and Asia Minor in Ignatius' time were familiar with the gifts of the Spirit. If Ignatius could speak as a prophet in Philadelphia, he probably ministered like that from time-to-time in his home church in Antioch, too. He does not seem to have regarded his prophetic speech in Philadelphia as something unusual, so perhaps we may assume that this kind of ministry was rather routine for him.

Furthermore, he could write to Polycarp, urging him to make the spiritual gifts a part of his ministry, apparently without being afraid that a charismatic bishop would be looked upon as strange by the Smyrnaeans or would further jeopardize the unity of that church.

The incident in Philadelphia when Ignatius spoke as a prophet reveals the high regard with which both Ignatius and the Philadelphians viewed prophecy. When the appropriateness of Ignatius' message aroused suspicion that someone had told him about the local situation, he insisted in defense of his action that the message had been spoken through him by the Holy Spirit. It looks as though this had the effect of removing the message from the sphere of human partiality and of lending it authority. The missing step in this argument is the idea that the Philadelphians would accept a word spoken by the prompting of the Spirit before they would accept something that some man had thought up. This same attitude is reflected in the charge which some Philadelphians seemed prepared to lay against Ignatius. If he really had prophesied, they would have to listen, but they suspected that he had faked prophecy for less than spiritual reasons.

Ignatius' position as a prophet-bishop is also of importance to the study of the growth of the clergy in the Christian Church: in him the authority of the bishop and the passion of the prophet were united. As we have seen, Did. 15:1 and 2 indicate that the local officials, bishops and deacons, in the communities to which the *Didache* was written were also carrying out the duties of prophets and teachers. Ignatius serves as a prime example of this marriage of administrative and charismatic service.

Ignatius, Bishop of Antioch, stands out of his letters as a man who supported whole-heartedly the concept of a well-recognized clergy with strong bishops at the head. However, at the same time, he emerges as a prophet, able to speak under the guidance of the Holy Spirit. This dual role is significant in that it shows that the Christian communities of Syria and Asia Minor were to some degree familiar with the gifts of the Spirit. It also reveals a stage in the development of the clergy in which the same individual was able to perform both administrative and charismatic functions. The information about charismatic ministry provided by our first early second century source is very important. Now, on to the second source.

The Shepherd of Hermas

As we go on to the next piece of relevant material, we again find ourselves moving from Syria to Rome. We now take up *The*

Shepherd of Hermas. This document is usually associated with the Roman church, but beyond that fairly securely fixed idea, uncertainty has reigned supreme over *The Shepherd.* What date should be assigned to the work has been a point of much contention,[5] but my opinion is that the combined impact of the various studies leads us into the early second century. There has been much discussion about how many revisions or authors the book as we have it was subject to. Further, the identity of Hermas, himself, and his role in the church at Rome have attracted much attention. We are pausing over this book here, because it presents material which suggests that prophecy was still to be found among Christians when it was written.

First, we must wrestle with information related to Hermas himself. Was he a prophet? In responding to that question, we have to acknowledge that there are numerous passages in the book in which visions which Hermas claimed to have received are described.[6] There are even two where he says he was commanded to publicize his visions (46:2 and 114:1-4). While Hermas does not actually insist that the title, "prophet," was rightfully his, he seems to have thought that he filled that role.

But was he really a prophet in the New Testament sense? Did his ministry conform to patterns which we find there? When we lay what we learn about the gift of prophecy in 1 Cor 12-14, some of the instances of New Testament prophecy (those found in Acts 13:2 and 21:11, for example) and even the experience of Ignatius at Philadelphia alongside Hermas, we immediately sense a difference. The relative simplicity and directness found in this biblical material and Ignatius is replaced in Hermas by a much more complex pattern. However, we must also bear in mind Peter's experience with visions which is recorded for us in Acts 10. There, God guided Peter by means of a vision. Therefore, Hermas' receiving visions is not without New Testament precedent.

Nevertheless, while Peter's experience is closer to Hermas than much of the other New Testament material, it must be admitted that there is still a significant distance between them. Hermas' visions are much more frequent and "grander" than Peter's, so much so that Hermas appears to have lapsed into a highly-subjective, essentially non-New Testament kind of mysticism. I am afraid that he may have gone so far that he has removed himself from the pattern of New Testament prophecy altogether, but I am hesitant to conclude that finally.

The second indication in *The Shepherd of Hermas* of the continuation of prophecy is more substantial than what we have just looked at. In 43:1-21, the question of true and false prophets is raised. The shepherd, who has been sent to instruct Hermas, points out that both types of prophets are around, and Hermas asks for a rule of thumb by which to distinguish one from the other. This the shepherd gives him, saying, "By his life you test the man that has the divine Spirit," and later, "You have before you the life of both kinds of prophets. By his deeds and life test, then, the man who says he is inspired."[7]

The first point which is of importance in this material is simply the fact that the distinction had to be made. If how you decide whether a prophet is true or false was an issue, there must have been a fair number of prophets around. H. B. Swete certainly thought that this was the case. "This," he says, "is remarkable testimony to the survival of prophecy in the Roman Church till perhaps the fourth or fifth decade of the second century."[8] Swete may be off with his dating of *The Shepherd,* but the point about the survival of prophecy is well-taken.[9]

It is also interesting to note how this passage says the true prophet functions. Herm. 43:9 says:

> So whenever the man who has the divine Spirit comes into an assembly of righteous men who have faith in the divine Spirit, and a prayer is made to God by the assembly of those men, then the angel of the prophetic spirit which is assigned to him fills the man, and that man, having been filled by the holy Spirit, speaks to the group as the Lord wills.[10]

There are a number of points to be underlined. First, the true prophet's ministry takes place in the context of group worship. It happens in "an assembly." Second, the prophet's message is directed to the group, not to an individual. Third, the prophet is filled by the Spirit and says what God wants him to say. He is not responding to someone's question the way this chapter in *The Shepherd* says the false prophet does. This picture of prophetic ministry has a great deal in common with what we find in 1 Cor 12-14. The clause "the angel of the prophetic spirit which is assigned to him fills the man" is an interesting addition, which is certainly not found in the Pauline material. However, that clause seems to parallel "having been filled by the Holy Spirit," although how the two fit together is not made clear by the shepherd or

Hermas. Nonetheless, something very similar to New Testament prophecy was well-known to Hermas and his contemporaries.

There is a great deal of controversy swirling around *The Shepherd of Hermas* and its author. However, Hermas was familiar with prophets and knew that they played a prominent role in the churches with which he was acquainted. In fact, Hermas may even have been a prophet in some sense himself. All of this combines to make him an important witness to the presence of the gifts of the Spirit among Christians in the early second century.

This period is one of relative darkness in the history of the Church. However, along with a very few other contributors, the experiences and the writings of Ignatius and Hermas cast some light over what was happening. Information we may gather from these two authors demonstrates that spiritual gifts were still found among Christians who lived at this time, and as we shall see, the gifts did not cease with them.

3

FROM SPIRIT AND MIND

As you move into the middle decades of the second century in a study of the Early Church, you find the lights coming back on. The Church had continued to grow in virtually every way. The number of Christians had multiplied dramatically; the social composition of the Church had shifted upward somewhat, and theology had developed. Christians were attempting to build logical systems which would accurately express what they believed. Authors came forward in increasing numbers, putting pen to paper in order to explain, defend, or teach the doctrines which would ultimately become the Christian "faith." The historian is able to speak with greater certainty about this period than he could about earlier times, because he has much more material to go on. The Church was alive and, for the most part, well, and it left a lot of tracks that the student can follow.

Some of the material which survives from the central part of the second century relates to the spirituality of the Christians who lived then. It helps us to get a "feel" for the religious climate that existed among at least some Christians, and it also suggests to us that the gifts of the Spirit continued to be a part of Christian experience. We will tap two sources of information, and again the movement will be from East to West.

The Odes of Solomon

The Odes have had a rather on-again-off-again relationship with the scholarly world. When Rendel Harris brought them out into the open again in 1909 after centuries in limbo, the theological world reacted with intense interest. Scholarly journals blossomed with articles on *The Odes* as researchers worked to free every possible ray of light which this hitherto lost collection of songs might be able to throw on the Early Church. They then dropped back out of sight for a couple of decades, only to float to the surface again in the late 1950s.

A great deal of detective work has been done in attempts to nail down such questions as where, when, and by whom were they written? in what language were they originally written? and do they reflect a heretical or orthodox Christian background? I wish to leave these questions aside and content myself with saying that I think they were written sometime before A.D. 150 in Syria by a person who belonged to the mainstream of the Christian Church.[1]

The Odes are important to this study because of what they are: the outpourings of a soul enraptured by God. R. M. Grant looks upon the odes as "individual 'psalms' like those mentioned in 1 Cor 14:26."[2] If he is correct, we are confronted by the words of someone who thought he was speaking in obedience to the promptings of the Holy Spirit. They show us that the Church from which they arose had people in it who were capable of getting excited about being caught up in God. As we glance at several of them, we will sense this spirit very readily.

Ode 11:6 and 7

And speaking waters drew near my lips
From the fountain of the Lord plenteously.

And I drank and was inebriated
With the living water that doth not die.[3]

John 7:38 and 39 refer to "living water" too, but in this passage from *The Odes* the phrase may mean something other than the Holy Spirit. I am reminded of the fountain named Castalia which was an essential part of the oracle of Apollo at Daphne in Syria. It was believed that the bubbling waters of this fountain gave off a "breath" which made the priests of the shrine delirious. They would then deliver messages from the god.

The odist is talking about an experience in which he felt the overpowering presence of God. Perhaps he is blending the pagan idea of water which has divine powers with the Christian concept of the Holy Spirit as "living water," but it is more likely that he is simply trying to express the rapture he felt.

Ode 12:1 and 2

He hath filled me with words of truth,
That I may speak the same.

And like the flow of waters, flows truth from my mouth,
And my lips show forth its fruits.

The prophetic awareness of these verses cannot be missed. The author is clearly claiming divine inspiration for his message.

Ode 18:4

O Lord, for the sake of them that are deficient,
Do not deprive me of thy word:

With regard to this ode, Harris comments,

The writer of this Psalm speaks as a prophet, who has known the Divine visitation, and has felt its effect both on mind and body, in the dispelling of error and the healing of disease. He prays for a continuance of the Heavenly gift for the sake of the needy people to whom he gives his message.[4]

The author of the ode is remembering times of past ministry, and he is asking for further empowering in order to be of assistance to others.

Ode 28:1 and 2

As the wings of the doves over their nestlings,
And the mouths of their nestlings toward their mouth,
So also are the wings of the Spirit over my heart.

My heart is delighted and leaps up,
Like the babe who leaps up in the womb of his mother.

Here the odist is attempting to convey the intensity of his desire to have communion with the Spirit and receive inspiration from Him.

Ode 36:1 and 2a

I rested on the Spirit of the Lord; and (the Spirit) raised me on high:

And made me to stand on my feet in the high place of the Lord.

The author is recalling an instance in which he had been drawn into ecstasy by the Spirit. This is the language of a prophet.

As well as the passages which have been quoted and commented upon above, there are several others which lend support to the idea that the odist was also a prophet. They are Odes 2:1 and 2; 7:18; 14:8; 16:5, and 40:2. All this material combines to give the picture of a man who was familiar with the virtually tangible moving of the Spirit, and it makes us assume that he must have ministered in an atmosphere which was receptive to that moving. Passion was not absent from the experience of God which second century Syrian Christians enjoyed. These people expected God to be actively involved in their lives.

The depth of the feeling displayed in *The Odes* is remarkable. The author's pleas for more of God make me think about what may have happened in Corinth after the Christians there had read Paul's first letter to them. He tells them to "earnestly desire the higher gifts" (1 Cor 12:31), to "make love your aim, and earnestly desire the spiritual gifts, especially that you may prophesy" (1 Cor 14:1), and to "strive to excel in building up the church" (1 Cor 14:12). I think the attitude toward the gifts of the Spirit which Paul wanted the Corinthians to have is illustrated clearly in *The Odes.* The religious climate which existed where *The Odes* were written must have been very favorable to the ministry of the gifts.

Justin Martyr

The movement from poetry to philosophy ought to be fairly easy: there have been many philosophical poets and poetic philosophers. Unfortunately, the transition cannot get by unnoticed in the case before us. We may be able to find some philosophy in *The Odes,* but, in my opinion, Justin is no poet! This aside, we have to bring him into focus, because he is of importance to this study.

Justin lived as a philosopher. We see him as a teen-ager, or at least a young man, searching for truth. He moved from one philosophical system to another, going through four before finally discovering satisfaction in Christianity. He was offended by one philosopher who seemed more interested in his fee than in philosophy, and he scornfully left him, while he, himself, was turned down by the representative of another school, because he could not meet the entrance requirements. However, in the end none of this mattered, because Justin was grasped by the true "philosophy," Christianity.

He never left philosophy. In fact, when he moved to Rome, he established a school at which he taught Christianity to all comers, presenting it as the only safe and profitable philosophical system.

Justin did not shut himself into the ivory tower, though. He became the model *par excellence* of the Christian apologist when he wrote a tract to the Emperor, his sons, and the Roman senate in which he pleads for fair treatment for Christians. In this book he tried to defuse the fear and suspicion which were arising all around the Christian Church. The attempt is a memorial to his concern, but it did not save its author. He died as a martyr for the Christian faith sometime between A.D. 162 and 168.

Justin occupies a unique position among early Christian authors, when you consider how he handles the topic of the gifts of the Spirit. As we have seen, and will see, a number of these people either experienced the gifts or made reference to them. However, Justin actually teaches about them. Granted, he does not say very much, but he makes a start. What he has to offer on this subject is found in his record of a theological discussion he had with a Jew named Trypho. The course of this conversation pulled theology out of Justin. We will first of all consider his comments and then try to assess their importance for our study.

The first material from Justin which we will look at is taken from chapter 39 of the *Dialogue with Trypho*:

> [some] are also receiving gifts, each as he is worthy, illumined through the name of this Christ. For one receives the spirit of understanding, another of counsel, another of strength, another of healing, another of foreknowledge, another of teaching, and another of the fear of God.[5]

In this chapter, Justin is reacting to the hatred with which the Jews of his time viewed Christianity. He had no illusions about their opinion of Christians. He seems to have seen some of the grounds for this feeling in the fact that every day people were leaving Jewish communities in order to become Christians. In passing he pointed out that some of these Jewish Christians were receiving gifts.

It is interesting to compare the list of gifts which Justin gives us here with those offered by Paul in Rom 12:6-8 and 1 Cor 12:8-11. When we do, we see that there are both similarities and differences. Two gifts, healing[6] and teaching,[7] appear in both Paul's and Justin's lists. Some similarity exists between other gifts which are mentioned in the lists, the "word of wisdom" and the "word of knowledge" in 1 Cor 12:8 and "understanding" and "foreknowledge" in *Dialogue*, 39. However, some of Justin's gifts, in particular, "counsel," "strength," and "the fear of God," do not obviously appear in either of Paul's lists. Nevertheless, taken all together, there is enough in common among these lists for us to assume that Paul and Justin are talking about the same things.

All of this is interesting, but the most important point about this passage from the *Dialogue* has not been noted yet. It says that Christians *are* receiving these gifts. This was happening at the time when Justin was writing.

The next piece of information in Justin's writings, which is of use to us in our study, is found right at the beginning of chapter 82—"For the prophetical gifts (Greek, *prophetika charismata*) remain with us, even to the present time."[8]

In the previous chapter, Justin had drawn support from Isaiah and from the Book of Revelation for certain ideas about the End Time that he had been arguing for. In the course of his discussion, he claimed that "there was a certain man among us," the Apostle John, who had prophesied. Justin seems to have thought that Trypho might be inclined to raise questions about John's ability to prophesy. To prevent this, Justin hurried on to point out that even in the present, some 50 or 60 years after John's death, there were Christians who prophesied. He also told Trypho very plainly that these gifts had been transferred to the Christians from the Jews.[9]

Justin expands on this last idea in chapters 87 and 88 of his *Dialogue*. Here he is responding to a question which had been put to him. Trypho refers to Isa 11:1 and 2.

> There shall come forth a shoot from the stump of Jesse, and a branch shall grow out of his roots.
>
> And the Spirit of the Lord shall rest upon him, the spirit of wisdom and understanding, the spirit of counsel and might, the spirit of knowledge and the fear of the Lord.
>
> And his delight shall be in the fear of the Lord.

Justin apparently had said that this passage found its fulfillment in Christ. What Trypho wanted to know was if Christ needed these gifts of the Spirit, how could He be regarded as preexistent. An absence of these abilities or characteristics would imply that Jesus was something less than fully divine.

The answer Justin gives is noteworthy. Christ did not receive these gifts because He needed them but rather because His having them was part of God's overall strategy for dealing with the Jews. It was God's intention to remove all gifts from the Jews, and He carried this out by giving them all to Christ. Then, in fulfillment of prophecy (Justin cites Ps 68:16 and Joel 2:28f.), Christ began to dispense these among Christians. Then, Justin brings his argument to its climax by saying, "It is possible to see amongst us women and men who possess gifts of the Spirit of God."[10]

The obvious goals of this material are to show why Christ received the gifts of the Holy Spirit and to explain what He then did with them. This is the first attempt in early Christian literature to account for the presence of the spiritual gifts in the Church. In the process of developing his thinking on this question, Justin, almost incidentally, provides evidence supporting the idea that spiritual gifts were still to be found among Christians of his day.

What Justin has to say about the gifts of the Spirit is fairly obvious. He thought they were still a part of Christian experience. But is what he says reliable? Do his comments about spiritual gifts accurately reflect conditions in the Church, at least at Rome, in the middle of the second century?

I think the answer is "yes." First, I would point out that historians studying the Early Church appear to have little difficulty in assuming Justin may be trusted when he talks about the Church of his time. For example, he has a lot to say about Christian worship and about the sacraments. Most people accept what he says as an accurate description of what was going on in the Roman church.[11] If Justin is trustworthy when he talks about some aspects of the mid-second century Roman church, his accuracy probably extends to other aspects too.

The reliability of Justin's comments about the gifts of the Spirit may be supported in other ways also. We should remember that we saw fairly strong hints of charismatic experience in Clement of Rome's letter to the Corinthians,[12] and we examined the evidence that *The Shepherd of Hermas* had to offer in support of the idea that Christians were experiencing the gifts of the Spirit.[13] Both of these sources of information are associated with the church of Rome, Justin's church. If their evidence is acceptable, it should not be surprising to find Christians there ministering by means of the gifts of the Spirit in Justin's time.

Before we leave Justin, there is something else we should consider. G.T. Purves says:

> Travelling, as he seems to have done, to the great cities of the Empire; residing, as he certainly did during many years, in the capital itself, and thus at the principal focus of the literary and religious as well as of the social and political activity of his day, he was likely to

know Christianity, not in its local peculiarities, but in its universal and essential features.[14]

This is very significant, if it is correct, and there seems to be good grounds for accepting Purves' comment. This means that when Justin makes general statements about the Church—as he does with reference to the gifts of the Spirit—perhaps he has in mind not only the church in Rome, but churches spread over a large geographical area.

Evidence drawn from Justin's *Dialogue with Trypho* goes a long way toward demonstrating that Christians of his time were no strangers to the ministry of the gifts of the Spirit.

As you follow the Church into the middle of the second century, your path becomes easier to see. More sources are available, and so more may be learned about what was happening then. We observe a lot of development in the organization of the Church, and we note the repeated attempts to arrive at an accurate idea of what Christian doctrine is. We also learn that there were those in the Church who were enjoying warm, active spiritual lives.

The Odes of Solomon is a window into someone's soul. What we see revealed is a passionate longing for the presence of God. The imagery highlights the reality of this vibrant religious life. Whatever the author of *The Odes* may have believed, here is one person, at least, who felt his Christianity deeply. His poetry may even be prophetic utterance.

Justin's writing style is much more down-to-earth, even dull. In spite of this, he leaves us thinking that the atmosphere of expectant adoration, which we feel in *The Odes,* is by no means unusual. On several occasions in the record of his conversation with Trypho, he refers to the gifts of the Spirit as though they were a part of the Church of his day. The one gives concrete evidence for things which happened in the atmosphere that we sense in the other. The Church of the mid-second century was charismatic. As we look further into its history, we will see that it continued to be so.

4

FROM THE CHURCH FRINGE

On moving into the second half of the second century, we find the atmosphere in the Church changing. Of course this change is not clear-cut or sudden. History flows like a river. It is all of one piece. What happens early is the foundation for what takes place later, and what occurs later is the outgrowth of earlier events. The Church did not change radically overnight, but when you compare what the Church was in the first half of this century to what it was in the second, a definite shift is noticeable. Perhaps what was going on may be described in one word—sophistication. The Church was growing up, and in doing so, it did not escape growing pains.

There are many tensions. Growth of organization, both on the local and the wide scale level, brought its struggles. Attempts to think through Christian doctrine aroused strife. People were asking basically similar questions but were coming up with unacceptably different answers. These and other factors led to an over-heated situation in which it became desperately important to find the truth and then stick to it, drawing a very clear line between yourself and those who were wrong.

While all of this was going on, God was still very much at work. Documents from the period indicate that the tide of spirituality was still flowing. Evidence that the gifts of the Spirit were still very important in the Church comes to us from a variety of directions during this period. We will focus here upon late second century Christian prophets and tongue speakers.

30

Montanism

The first well (some would unhesitatingly say "cesspool") from which we draw information is Montanism. Holding very firmly in mind material found in several passages from Eusebius and Epiphanius, I think we can best date the appearance of this movement to shortly after A.D. 170.[1] Right from the time when it first came to the surface, Montanism has received very mixed reviews.[2] There is no doubt that these people had some rather strange ideas, but it seems to me that it is hard to justify the popular idea that Montanism was one of the major heresies threatening the Early Church.

For many, Montanism equals Tertullian, the famous North African Christian author. I want to bypass that equation and go back to the earlier Montanism of Asia Minor. On one hand, for reasons we will glance at later, I think there are some pretty far-reaching questions to be asked about Tertullian's relationship with Montanism. On the other hand, Asian Montanism has a great deal of significance in its own right. We are able to get to it by means of its prophecies which have come down to us, comments made by its contemporaries, and inscriptions found in the area where it was strongest, and we will be well rewarded for making the effort to study it.

Montanism arises from the material related to it as a very provocative religious movement. Questions are asked about its doctrinal position. Its attitude toward martyrdom, its thinking about the End Time, its code of ethics, and the organization of its ministry are of interest. All of this becomes particularly pressing as you try to find out why the movement was eventually pronounced heretical. However, what will occupy us here will be only one facet of the movement, albeit its most characteristic and controversial one, its practice of spiritual gifts. We will take two steps, observing as we go that prophecy among the Montanists had a lot in common with how the Church at large viewed it and that the Montanists probably spoke in tongues, too.

When we launch into a study of the gifts of the Spirit among the Montanists, we turn to the sixteen prophecies from them which have survived. With these in hand, let us first try to find out what the inner condition of the Montanist prophet was while he was prophesying.

A prophecy preserved by Epiphanius provides us with a jumping off point:

Behold, a man is like a lyre and I pluck his
strings like a pick;
The man sleeps, but I am awake.
Behold, it is the Lord, who is changing the
hearts of men and giving new hearts to them.[3]

We can pick up the main point of this passage fairly easily. It
tells us that when a prophet is prophesying, God is in complete
control. This idea is emphasized by borrowing an image from the
world of music. In order for instrumental music to be produced
there must, of course, be an instrument in playable condition: its
keys, strings, valves, or skins are essential. However, before sound
comes from that instrument it must be touched by a musician. His
fancy determines whether or not the instrument will be played and
what type of music will be produced on it. Similarly, for there to be
prophecy, there must be someone willing to prophesy, but when he
does so and what he says depends completely upon God.

The second verse in the passage underlines what we have just
seen. God is pictured as acting through a man who is asleep. This
stresses the passiveness of the prophet during prophecy—it is as
though his natural faculties were asleep. He does not compose his
message nor plan his actions. God works through him.

Therefore, as far as the Montanists were concerned, during
prophecy the prophet is passive. God controls him and delivers the
message He wants people to hear through him.

When we look at the content of some of these messages delivered
"under the control of God," what we have just observed is
hammered in a little deeper. In the prophecies which have been
preserved, there is a recurring theme having to do with the
relationship between the prophet and God. This is found in the
prophecies contained in Epiphanius' *Panarion,* 48:11 (2 prophecies
here), 48:12, Eusebius' *Ecclesiastical History,* 5, 16:17, Tertullian's
On Modesty, 21, and Didymus' *On the Trinity,* 3:41. The common
denominator of all these passages is that in every one, one member
of the Trinity or another (or all of them) is assumed to have been in
the Montanist concerned and to have spoken through him (or her).
Two prophecies illustrate this particularly well.

For Montanus spoke, saying, "I am the father, and the son and the
paraclete."[4]

You shall not hear from me, but you have heard from Christ.[5]

In the first of these prophecies, Montanus, the leader of the movement, was involved, and in the second, it was one of his associates, Maximilla.

It seems true to say, then, that among the Montanists prophecy was a type of ecstasy in which God was in control of the prophet. This is certainly a departure from the Pauline pattern in 1 Cor 14:29-31, where prophets are able to control themselves. Where did this concept of prophecy come from, then?

We have to start by acknowledging that this was how prophecy was regarded in pagan circles at that time. Literature from that part of society is dotted with references to "god-possession," and what is described there is very similar to what we see in Montanism.

However, we do not have to go that far in order to come up with an explanation for what the Montanists thought about prophecy. For instance, it is useful to remind ourselves of the way Christians of the second century understood Old Testament prophecy. Several of the Greek apologists belong to this period, and their works give us some help. Justin claims that the Spirit spoke through the prophets and the psalmist;[6] Theophilus flatly states that the Old Testament prophets were possessed by God,[7] and Athenagoras says regarding Moses, Isaiah, Jeremiah, and other Old Testament figures that they were

> lifted in ecstasy above the natural operations of their minds by the impulses of the Divine Spirit, [and that they] uttered the things with which they were inspired, the Spirit making use of them as a flute player breathes into a flute.[8]

The emphasis in these passages is upon the activity of God and the passiveness of the prophet. These men viewed Old Testament prophecy in much the same way that their non-Christian contemporaries looked upon pagan prophets. It must be admitted, of course, that these three Christians had come to the Church through the Greek world of their time, and, no doubt, they had absorbed many of its ideas. However, in the light of their educational backgrounds, they were probably among the least gullible members of the Christian community. They were probably also among those who would be the most critical of the pagan world around them. If they held a view of Old Testament prophecy that was similar to the contemporary understanding of pagan prophecy, it is fairly likely that many other Christians did also.

The Greek apologists give us some idea of what the mainstream of the second century Christian Church thought about prophecy, and their thinking is very similar to what we found among the Montanists. In fact, Athenagoras even used an illustration from music in the same way that Montanus did.

We can even advance beyond this point. Not only can we compare Montanist and mainstream Christian thinking about prophecy, but we can also look at the inner experience of prophets in both groups. Unfortunately, there is no example of a non-Montanist Christian prophet coming from the second half of the second century, but we can turn to Ignatius, who lived some sixty years earlier.

When we were studying Ignatius,[9] we saw that he was a prophet-bishop and that, on at least one occasion, he claimed to have served as a mouthpiece for God. On that occasion, he denied that the message which he had delivered was his, insisting that God had spoken through him. This is very similar to what we found in the prophecies of Montanus and Maximilla, which we quoted earlier.[10]

All of this demonstrates that the Montanist view and experience of prophecy had a lot in common with what was happening in the Church at large. The Montanists had moved somewhat from the picture that Paul presented in 1 Corinthians 14, but they certainly were not alone: the Church was there, too. Perhaps both had been influenced by the way prophets acted in the pagan world around them.

Now that we have examined the Montanist prophecies in an attempt to find out what they say about the nature of the experience, we are ready to take our second step. Let us turn to what the critics of early Montanism had to say in order to see if they add anything. As soon as we make the turn, we see that the spirituality of the Montanists was more complex than it has appeared up to this point.

On one hand, there are Montanist prophecies which, in so far as language goes, are clear, readily understandable statements. For example, we hear Maximilla saying, "I am driven away like a wolf from the sheep. I am not a wolf, I am word and spirit and power."[11] Whatever we may think about the sentiments expressed, we can understand the words. They are not obscure. Anyone who knew Greek and who was standing by would have understood her.

On the other hand, there are three passages in Apolinarius' refutation of Montanism, as preserved by Eusebius, in which the Montanists are described as speaking in a most unusual, difficult to understand way. How do we explain this apparent variety of speech? Let us look more closely at these three passages from Apolinarius.

The first is "He began to be ecstatic and to speak and to talk strangely."[12] Montanus' ecstasy, his being filled by God, resulted in unusual speech. Secondly, we read, ". . . so that they (Maximilla and another colleague, Priscilla) spoke madly and improperly and strangely, like Montanus."[13] Both of these passages emphasize the strangeness of the Montanists' speech.

The last passage is really just a fragment: ". . . because we did not receive their chattering prophets."[14] The key word is "chattering." This is how Lake translated the Greek word *ametrophōnous*, but others have handled it differently. McGiffert renders it as "loquacious,"[15] and Oulton's treatment of the whole phrase produces "prophets of unbridled tongues."[16] These translators have come up with different words, but they agree closely about the meaning: the Montanist prophets spoke at great length or very often.

However, there is no objective check which you can apply to the translations of this passage, because this is the only place in Greek literature where the word *ametrophōnous* appears.[17] When you run into a situation like this the only thing you can do is have a good look at the possible meanings of the smaller words which make up the word you are concerned with and then decide which combination of these meanings best suits the context in which the word is found.

Having done this, I suggest that we translate the phrase so that it means prophets "who speak in an indefinite number of what sounds like languages." That translation will not win any prizes for beauty, but it is a possible rendering of the phrase. It indicates that we may have here a reference to tongue speaking. If it is, we would have an explanation for the two different types of speech we find in Montanism. Perhaps they were involved with both prophecy and tongues. Is that possible? I think it is even probable.[18]

Montanism broke upon the Church in Asia Minor, disrupting its life, in the early A.D. 170s. Once it had recovered from the initial shock, the Church set about to cut short the life of this "heresy of the Phrygians." What the Church seems to have been most concerned about in Montanism was a type of ecstatic utterance which the Montanist thought resulted from being possessed by God. This kind of prophetic activity shared much with pagan religious experience, but it was also close to what was being thought and experienced in mainstream Christianity. A careful study of the texts of the Montanist prophecies and of comments made by early critics of the movement points strongly to the conclusion that prophecy and tongues, two spiritual gifts prominent within the New Testament Church, had continued among Christians into the second half of the second century.

Celsus

The next piece of material we will draw into our study comes to us from a rather strange direction. Toward the end of his career, Origen, the famous theologian, was asked by a friend to respond to an attack that had been launched on Christianity by a Platonist philosopher, Celsus. Some seventy years earlier, around A.D. 180, Celsus had attempted to explore Christianity's weaknesses. Origen's book, *Against Celsus,* is his response to this request. His method was to cite passages from the book which contained Celsus' attack, *True Discourse,* commenting upon them critically.

One of the passages Origen quotes is of interest to us here, because it suggests that Celsus had come across something which resembled charismatic gifts rather closely. We will look at the passage in question carefully, trying to see exactly what it was that Celsus was talking about, and then we will attempt to identify the people whom Celsus had met.

The passage with which we are concerned is found in *Against Celsus,* 7,9:

> There are many, he says, who become enraptured and prophesy very easily on any grounds, both in temples and outside of temples, and there are some who—begging and visiting cities and camps periodically—are gesticulating and posturing as if they are prophesying. And it is convenient and customary for each one to say, "I am God, or a son of God, or a divine spirit. And I have come. For the world is already perishing, and you, O men, are dying because of wickedness. But I want to save you. And you shall see me returning hereafter with heavenly power. Blessed is he who has now worshipped me. Upon all others I shall cast eternal fire, on both cities and country regions. And men who do not know their penalties shall repent and groan in vain. But I shall preserve eternally those who believe in me." . . . To these things which were held up before men were added unheard of raving and entirely unknown speech, the meaning of which no rational man was able to determine; for being obscure and meaningless they allow any irrational person or cheat to make of the words whatever he wishes.[19]

5
FROM BISHOPS

The deposit of source material to which the historian may turn as he studies the Church during the period from around A.D. 150 to about 200 is rich when compared to what he has to go on in the earlier decades. As we pursue a study of the gifts of the Spirit in this chapter, we remain in the second half of the second century. We have by no means exhausted the relevant material by looking at the Montanist movement and Celsus.

However, our focus does shift somewhat. When we were working with the sources which we used in the previous chapter, we were hovering on the edge of the second century Church. Whether or not I think the Montanists were *bona fide* Christians, many of their contemporaries most certainly did not. As far as a significant portion of the Church was concerned, the Montanists were the "lunatic fringe," or worse. And anything of benefit that you might pick up from Celsus would have to be rather backhanded to say the least; not the sort of stuff you would stake your life on. Could you expect it to be otherwise when you are dealing with someone who apparently hated the Church?

All of that changes now. We move from the fringe to the very center of the Church. The people to whom we turn had status among their contemporaries, and not all that many peers. They were tried, proven, and by most people, respected leaders—bishops, even. I am talking about Irenaeus and Eusebius of Caesarea. They, too, provide significant amounts of information about the

41

spiritual lives of Christians in the latter part of the second century. In fact, their material helps us to see that the gifts of the Spirit were very important features of Christianity during the period in question. We will first consult Irenaeus and then move on to Eusebius.

Irenaeus

This Bishop of Lyons is a key figure in our study. He occupies this position because he offers some important data about the gifts of the Spirit in the Church of his time. However, before we turn to the evidence we want to consider, we should try to get the measure of the man, that is, find out who and what he really was. This initial step is essential if we are going to evaluate accurately what he says about the gifts of the Spirit.

We begin by acknowledging that we do not know exactly when he was born or when he died. However, we do have many other facts about him at our disposal.

He was probably born in Asia Minor, a theological hotbed in the second century, insofar as he came under the influence of the venerable Polycarp, Bishop of Smyrna, in his youth. However, he played out most of his life in the Roman province of Gaul, now France. We are not sure when he emigrated, but he appears to have associated himself with a church in southeastern Gaul, which was made up primarily of people from the East, like himself. He comes to the surface in A.D. 177 as a priest in the church at Lyons.

He was not just an ordinary priest, either. By the time he is first mentioned, his superior ability had already been recognized. We find him serving as a special envoy on behalf of Gallic Christians, carrying letters to the bishop of Rome. He had shown himself to be trustworthy and committed. The stuff of leadership was in him.

This strength of character was to find full expression when, after the martyrdom of Pothinus, he was chosen to be bishop of Lyons. In this position, he became the shepherd of a sprawling diocese which included the churches of Lyons and Vienne and parishes scattered throughout southern Gaul.

These facts combine to create the picture of a man who had a broad knowledge of the Church of his time. Irenaeus had seen the Church in both East and West, and in both urban and rural settings. These extensive contacts with Christians in various places must have given him an outlook which was more global than regional. For example, he knew about the controversy in far-off

Asia Minor swirling around Montanus and his followers. The letters he carried to Rome dealt with that. There is certainly no reason to believe that he lost this perspective once he had become a bishop.

Once Irenaeus assumed responsibility as bishop, another side of him appeared. He devoted himself to the defense of the true doctrine of the Church. False ideas about the Christian faith would not find place among his flock as long as he held the shepherd's crook. Of his many writings, two survive—*The Demonstration of the Apostolic Teaching* and *Against Heresies*—and in both of them he is attacking various strains of Gnosticism.[1] Irenaeus stands out of these works as a full-fledged Christian theologian—probably the first of a new breed of men. I wonder how carefully he went about his work. What kind of a scholar was he?

This question may be answered by pausing over the *Against Heresies*. Until the middle of the present century, this work was the major source of information regarding certain second century schools of thought which have been lumped together under the name "Gnosticism." Over the years new material has come to light which has made it possible to assess how accurately Irenaeus understood the groups he opposed. Along with other documents, the Coptic Gnostic library discovered in 1945 or 1946 near Nag Hammadi in Egypt forms a large body of Gnostic literature against which Irenaeus can be checked.

When this examination took place, Irenaeus passed with honors. It was discovered that what he had to say corresponded well with what is to be found in the Gnostic texts. While discussing this question, Professor R. McL. Wilson says:

> The general reliability of Irenaeus, our earliest major witness, has been abundantly vindicated by the researches of Foerster and Sagnard, and the conclusions of these scholars are now amply confirmed by such of the Nag Hammadi documents as have been published.[2]

This means that when Irenaeus decided to examine Gnosticism, he succeeded in getting to know it well. We can place confidence in him when he is talking about Gnosticism.

So, not only was Irenaeus a leader with a broad perspective on the affairs of the Church, but he was also a man with relatively careful scholarly habits. This suggests to me that when Irenaeus makes comments about what was going on around him among

Christians, he deserves to be listened to with respect.

With this examination of the character and life of Irenaeus behind us, we can now turn our attention to the evidence he offers to a study of the spiritual gifts in the Early Church.

There are two passages in *Against Heresies* in which he lists gifts of the Spirit which he knows exist in the Church. The first of these is:

> . . . for which cause also his [Christ's] true disciples having received grace from him use it in his name for the benefit of the rest of men, even as each has received the gift from him. For some drive out demons with certainty and truth, so that often those who have themselves been cleansed from the evil spirits believe and are in the church, and some have foreknowledge of things to be, and visions and prophetic speech, and others cure the sick by the laying on of hands and make them whole, and even as we have said, the dead have been raised and remained with us for many years. And why should I say more? It is not possible to tell the number of the gifts which the church throughout the whole world, having received them from God in the name of Jesus Christ, who was crucified under Pontius Pilate, uses each day for the benefit of the heathen, deceiving none and making profit from none. For as it received freely from God, it ministers also freely.[3]

Irenaeus is arguing against certain heretics who have claimed to have souls of the same kind as that of Jesus and who at times have claimed to be superior to him (*Against Heresies*, 2, 49:2). Irenaeus says that their works have been of benefit to no one. He then points to the great works which are performed in Jesus' name and which prove that he is greater than the men in question. Irenaeus is not primarily dealing with the past here. Throughout most of the list he gives, it is clear that Irenaeus is talking about ways in which Christ ministers to mankind through the Church in the present.

He provides a list of spiritual gifts which were to be seen in the Church, and it is an impressive one. It includes such gifts as the ability to cast out demons, knowledge about the future, visions, and prophetic speech. The list given by Irenaeus has obvious similarities to those found in Romans 12 and 1 Corinthians 12. Both Irenaeus' and Paul's lists talk about prophecy and healing, and both include a gift that has to do with the control of evil spirits: with Paul, the ability to distinguish among spirits; with Irenaeus, exorcism.

However, for our purposes, the significance of this passage from the *Against Heresies* lies not only in the parallels to the Pauline lists it has, but also, and primarily, in the fact that it says at least some of the gifts of the Spirit were being seen in Irenaeus' day.

Up to this point, I have said nothing about one of the items which Irenaeus included in his list of gifts. He says, "and even as we have said, the dead have been raised and remained with us for many years." If that was in fact going on, that is striking information, to say the least. However, I am skeptical enough to question it. But does not questioning what Irenaeus says about this cast a shadow over the reliability of the whole passage? Not really.

This is a question to which Benjamin Warfield addressed himself.[4] He draws attention to two features of this statement that suggest that Irenaeus did not want his readers to think that dead people had been raised recently. First, he points to a blunt shift in the tenses of the verbs in the passages. All of the other gifts are referred to in the present tense, but raising the dead is introduced in the past tense. Further, he underlines the fact that, after the dead in question had been brought back to life, they remained alive for a considerable number of years. This obviously means that quite a bit of time had passed since they had been raised. Warfield concludes by saying that "there is no reason why the cases he [Irenaeus] has in mind may not have occurred during the lifetime of the Apostles or of Apostolic men," and I think he is right.

The second passage I want to look at is *Against Heresies,* 5, 6:1:

> Just as also we hear many brethren in the church who have gifts of prophecy, and who speak through the Spirit with all manner of tongues, and who bring the hidden things of men into the clearness for the common good and expound the mysteries of God.[5]

This material comes up in the midst of a discussion on spiritual perfection. Again there is a brief list of spiritual gifts, and again there are contacts between this list and Paul's.

This is an eyewitness testimony to the fact that the gifts of the Spirit were active in the Church, and this is what makes this selection important. Irenaeus goes on record, saying that the Church he knows is charismatic. He actually refers to people whom he has heard ministering through prophecy, etc. He seems to be going out of his way to demonstrate that the miraculous power of God had not departed from the Church.

How are we to regard this material from Irenaeus? Can we accept what he says? I think we can. Let us remember what was said earlier about Irenaeus. He was a man who had close contact with a wide segment of the Christian Church, and he had status within it. He was a respected leader. As far as his scholarship goes, the Nag Hammadi find has helped to demonstrate that he was concerned about factual accuracy. He made sure he was telling it like it was. As far as I am concerned, he was a man whose word may be accepted, not blindly, but with a large measure of confidence. I think that what he says shows pretty clearly that the gifts of the Spirit were still around in the Christian Church of his time.

Eusebius of Caesarea

The second bishop we will listen to for awhile is none other than Eusebius of Caesarea, perhaps the first committed historian that the Church produced. Incidentally, he agrees with my assessment of Irenaeus' comments,[6] but he is of interest in his own right.

Eusebius seems to have led a long and vigorous life, dying perhaps in A.D. 340. He was a prominent figure in the church of his day, an intimate friend of the great Constantine, the first Christian emperor, whom Eusebius seemed to think stood only the thickness of a thumbnail below God himself! He was deeply enmeshed in the plotting and counter-plotting that boiled up as the Arian controversy, which occupied so much of the Church's time during the first half of the fourth century. Whatever Eusebius' theology was, and there were a lot of questions asked about that, he was a man with a keen interest in the past, one who went to great bother to gather historical material. The fruits of his work are still invaluable to students of the Early Church.

Eusebius brought the results of this historical research together in his *Ecclesiastical History,* a monumental work which he put into its final form around A.D. 320. There is one passage in this book which is particularly important for our study. In it Eusebius expresses an opinion about what was going on with regard to the spiritual gifts in the latter period of the second century. We are going to have a look at this material, trying to find out exactly what Eusebius said and to assess its value as evidence of charismatic ministry. However, before we do this it would be worthwhile to see if we can judge Eusebius' historical work generally.

It is fairly obvious that his basic thinking about history was sound. He recognized the importance of getting to material which came from the period he wanted to study. This led him to work very hard at gathering it. His *Ecclesiastical History* is liberally seasoned with quotations from a wide range of writings, which makes it a gold mine of information about the thought of men who are unknown outside of its pages.

However, in spite of his passion for good sources, Eusebius had some hang-ups which put question marks over much of his historical work.[7] He was a prejudiced man. His theological convictions got in the way of his historical fairness, and nowhere is this more true than where he is dealing with heresy or persecutors. In the case of those who had distorted the true faith, he never allows them to speak for themselves but always filters their ideas through "orthodox" writers. He treats the dates of heretical groups so as to make them appear as young as possible, thus reducing the credibility of their claims to be true successors to the Apostles.

Eusebius also lacked critical ability. We see this in the way he accepts contradictory conclusions from time-to-time. This lack made him rather gullible.

Finally, there is a certain degree of carelessness in Eusebius' work. It seems that he frequently quoted his sources from memory. He may also have delegated the task of copying out quotations to assistants and then failed to check their work. Whatever the explanations are, some of the quotations are rather butchered.

There is little doubt that if Eusebius were trying to make a place for himself in the historical world today, these flaws would make it difficult for him to get his Ph.D. thesis accepted! However, in spite of this, his work continues to be of great value, if only as a source of historical data which we simply would not have had without him.

Now we can turn to *Ecclesiastical History*, 5, 3:4, the passage relevant to our study:

> Just then the Montanus, Alcibiades, and Theodotus party in Phrygia was spreading its idea of prophecy among many for the first time (for there were still many other marvelous works of the gifts of God being done in different churches up to that time which gave rise to the belief among many that these men also were prophets).[8]

Here Eusebius is offering an explanation for the rapid growth of Montanism, which occurred in the early A.D. 170s, and, even though it is in parentheses, it is important. He thinks that the warm reception which Montanist prophecy received, in places at least, can be accounted for by the fact that at that time many churches were still familiar with spiritual gifts. Christians expected to see unusual things happen among them, so they had little difficulty with Montanus and his friends.

There are some problems with the passage as it stands. Eusebius says there were *"many (pleistai)* other marvelous works"* around in the churches. Can we take that "many" seriously? Perhaps it is just window dressing tacked up to improve appearances. Walter Bauer thinks so.[9]

Furthermore, most unfortunately, Eusebius does not give us a footnote in which the source of his information is identified. (Not even an undergraduate could get away with that today!) Is this a raw guess? Did he have concrete sources? Is this a general impression he had picked up? Can we accept what he says?

Most of these questions we cannot answer. However, I think that, regardless of whether Eusebius was guessing, sharing a general impression, or going on bedrock fact, he hit the nail on the head.

Evidence for the presence of the gifts of the Spirit among Christians during this part of the second century is plentiful. Even leaving Montanism aside, we have been able to review material from *The Odes of Solomon,* Justin, Celsus, Irenaeus, and we are going to go on to look at a couple of other sources as well. Obviously not all this evidence is of the same value. *The Odes,* for example, are not nearly as helpful as Irenaeus is. However, the overall picture which comes together is significant. Look at the geographical spread involved: *The Odes of Solomon* and Celsus, Palestine and Syria; Justin, Rome; Irenaeus, France, and we noted that what Justin and Irenaeus have to say probably applies to many places other than just where they lived.

I think we can say that Christians of the later decades of the second century were no strangers to the gifts of the Spirit. If that is true, Eusebius' comment fits very well, and we can grant his accuracy.

Up to this point in our study of the gifts of the Spirit in the Church of the second half of the second century, we had looked at a poet, a philosopher, a group of so-called heretics, and an arch-critic of Christianity. Here we have turned to men of power, bishops, Irenaeus and Eusebius. What they have done is add significantly to the body of evidence which supports the idea that Christians of this time continued to be charismatic. Irenaeus comments upon what he sees going on around him, while Eusebius looks back over about 140 years. They both point clearly to the ongoing importance of spiritual gifts.

6

FROM HERESY AND SUPERSTITION

It has been comfortable hobnobbing with bishops for awhile. But now as we approach the end of second century material related to a study of spiritual gifts, we swerve sharply away from them and dive into murky waters. The material we are going on to is somewhat difficult to handle, coming as it does out of Gnosticism and the Apocryphal Acts. However, I am trying to provide a comprehensive picture of charismatic experience in the Early Church, and the documents to which we will be turning were part and parcel of that Church. We will have to deal with the information where we find it.

Excerpts from Theodotus

As we saw earlier, Irenaeus devoted a lot of energy to attacking various Gnostic systems which he found threatening the Church —and threatening it they were. The danger the Church faced was real. Perhaps ironically, there are hints of deep spirituality within these groups, as well as within the mainstream of the Church.

We find a clue pointing in this direction in the work of Theodotus, a member of the eastern branch of Valentinianism. Much of his material is preserved in Clement of Alexandria's *Excerpta ex Theodoto*. In 24:1 we read,

> The Valentinians say that the excellent Spirit which each of the prophets had for his ministry was poured out upon all those of the church. Therefore the signs of the Spirit, healings and prophecies, are being performed by the church.[1]

49

It is a little hard to see exactly what Theodotus wanted to say in this brief passage. Maybe he was attempting to establish an identity between the Spirit who inspired the (I assume, Old Testament) prophets and the Spirit who had been poured out upon the Church. From the fact that prophecy and healings were still to be found in the Church, things which had marked the ministries of the prophets, Theodotus might be arguing that it was the same Spirit who stood behind these in both eras.

On the other hand, perhaps he is trying to provide an explanation for certain features of his own circumstances, namely, the spiritual gifts. He could be saying that they are to be regarded as the results of the continued activity of the Spirit who had performed miracles through the prophets of the Old Testament.

However, regardless of what the main thrust of this passage is, it seems to show that the gifts of the Spirit were known in the circles in which Theodotus moved.

In order to catch the impact of the passage more completely, we have to ask what Theodotus and the Valentinians meant by "church," (*ecclēsia*). Clement does not seem to think that they give it any special meaning. In *Excerpta* 24:1, he quotes them as they use the word twice, and then in *Excerpta* 24:2 he, himself, employs the word, saying nothing about any possible difference of meaning. Either "church" was used in the same sense by the Valentinians and the more orthodox sections of the Church, or Clement was unaware of the distinction.

In fact, however, F. Sagnard does argue that the Valentinians did apply a distinctive meaning to "church." He says that for them the word meant the assembly of the elect, of those who had been initiated into their special knowledge or gnosis. This they thought was different from the rest of the non-Valentinian Church.[2] In the eyes of a Valentinian, the "church" was composed of Valentinians only.

If Sagnard is right, this passage has some interesting implications. It would seem to be saying that the gifts of healing and prophecy were to be found in the eastern Valentinian community in the third quarter of the second century. We have to admit that the spiritual gifts were not an important feature in Gnosticism, this is the only reference to them in the Gnostic literature. However, it looks as though they may have been there.

The Apocryphal Acts

By the third quarter of the first century, the Church was beginning to commit her thoughts and records to writing. The first generation of the followers of Jesus had been willing to leave their traditions in a largely oral form, but circumstances necessitated a change in policy. Time was passing. The coming of the Lord was delayed. Christians began to realize that if they were to retain a record of the life and words of their Master and of His early followers, they must write. Furthermore, the rapid spread of the new faith made it impossible for the community's leaders to be physically present everywhere to guide development. They must write. Thus the Church was led into the literary field, and under the guidance of the Holy Spirit, it quickly learned to employ this medium to its advantage.

Many of the documents produced in Christian communities in the first three centuries were concerned with giving information about Jesus and His Apostles. The passage of time helped the Church to see that some of the documents it had in its hands were of greater value than others. The greater ability of these materials to edify, plus apostolic authorship, led to their being given a larger place in the Christian community than was granted to the others. These favored writings became the canonical books, while those held in less favor came to be regarded as noncanonical or apocryphal.

It looks as though one of the books destined for the Canon, The Acts of the Apostles, prompted the production of other books: the Apocryphal Acts. These Acts tried to add to what the canonical Acts said about the individual apostles, and they tried to show how the apostles fought heresies; not heresies that were present during the apostolic age, but heresies that existed at the time when these new acts were written.

As time passed, these Acts became more and more romanticized. As I read them I find myself transported to a fantasy world that makes me think of King Arthur and his court or the Arabian Nights. And, of course, the more fictional the Acts became, the less valuable they are as historical documents. We really cannot accept much, if anything, of what they say as true. However, B. M. Metzger makes a comment which keeps us from dismissing the Apocryphal Acts too quickly. He says:

Yet the New Testament Apocrypha are important documents in their own way. True enough, as historical sources of the Apostolic age they are negligible. The permanent value of this body of literature lies in another direction, namely in reflecting the beliefs of their authors and the tastes of their early readers who found profit as well as entertainment in tales of this kind. That is, the New Testament Apocrypha are important as historical documents which tell us much, not about the age with which they profess to deal, but about the age which gave them birth. They purport to be reliable accounts of the words and deeds of the Apostles; in reality they set forth under the names of the Apostles certain ideals of Christian life and conceptions of Christian faith current in the second and succeeding centuries.[3]

When we look upon the Apocrypha in this way, they become an effective means of getting inside the minds of the authors and their contemporaries, and to a lesser extent, inside their religious experience. The importance of the Apocrypha lie not in what they say happened, but in what the authors and readers thought could happen.

How can the Apocrypha help us here? I want to look at it to see if these people had any inkling of what the gifts of the Spirit were all about. When we do look, we discover that they did. In fact, there are several features in their descriptions of their heroes and their deeds which remind us of the spiritual gifts.

First, we discover that there are several instances in the Apocryphal Acts when special knowledge is given to an apostle. This occurs twice in the case of Paul. Once he is told that a woman who had come to receive the Lord's Supper had come out of a moral situation which made her unworthy to participate.[4] On another occasion, a young man had fallen to his death while Paul was preaching. The man had been Nero's cup-bearer and messengers were immediately sent to the emperor. Paul perceived this turn of events "in the spirit."[5]

The Apostle John is also portrayed as having had this sort of experience. At one time, John was able to announce to a congregation what one of its members had done and thought before he came into the service,[6] and at another, he was able to read a man's thoughts.[7]

All four of these instances could be interpreted as the actions of a clairvoyant, but the way in which the authors present them points in another direction. In each case, the special knowledge the apostle received was closely associated with the Spirit. It came as they were "filled with the Spirit" or were "in the Spirit." The authors seem to be trying to get the idea across as clearly as possible that the Holy Spirit can give knowledge. This sounds like an echo of 1 Cor 12:8, where the word of knowledge is spoken of.

The second kind of experience we will look at involves the oral delivery of a message after someone has come in contact with the Holy Spirit. In the *Acts of Paul* there are three times when a person is "filled with the Spirit" and then goes on to deliver a powerful message. In section 9, Paul is filled and exhorts the brethren;[8] in the same passage, Cleobius is filled and speaks of Paul's death,[9] and in section 11, 3, Paul is filled and speaks with power before Nero.[10]

There is another passage which presents a variation of the same idea:

> But the Spirit came upon Myrta, so that she said: "Brethren, why [are you alarmed at the sight of this sign?] Paul the servant of the Lord will save many in Rome, and will nourish many with the word, so that there is no number (to count them), and he (?) will become manifest above all the faithful, and greatly will the glory [. . . come] upon him, so that there will be great grace in Rome." And immediately, when the Spirit that was in Myrta was at peace, each one took of the bread and feasted according to custom [. . .] amid the singing of psalms of David and of hymns.[11]

Here the author presents Myrta as speaking under the control of the Spirit. The author here seems to want all of these passages to be regarded as Christian prophecy.

A Coptic papyrus containing "The Beginning of the Stay in Ephesus" from the *Acts of Paul* provides what may be regarded as a third type of spiritual experience. There we read:

> The angel of the Lord came into the house of Aquila, and stood before them all. He spoke with Paul, so that all were troubled: for [this angel] who stood there was indeed visible (lit. revealed), but the words which he was speaking to Paul they (the bystanders) did not hear. But after he had stopped speaking with Paul in tongues, they fell into fear and confusion, and were silent. But Paul looked at the brethren and said: . . .[12]

What we should focus upon are the words "speaking in tongues." Here an angel is pictured speaking and Paul seems to interpret what he said. This reference to tongues, and possibly interpretation, has a lot in common with what we come across in 1 Cor 12-14. It is interesting to see that the speech in tongues is put on the lips of an angel. Maybe the author was influenced by Paul's statement in 1 Cor 13:1, "If I speak with the tongues of men and of angels."

Fourthly, there are several passages in the Apocryphal Acts which portray confrontations between the various apostles and demons. We will look at two. The first incident takes place in the house of Marcellus in Rome. There Peter sees a young man and perceives that he is demon-possessed. He commands, "You too, then, whatever demon you may be, in the name of our Lord Jesus Christ, come out of the young man and do him no harm; (and) show yourself to all who stand by!"[13] Handcuffed by the apostle's authority, the demon leaves the young man and proceeds to destroy a marble statue of the emperor (that helped the readers see who *really* had the power in the Empire, and it certainly was not the emperor!).

The second example of this sort of experience comes to us from the *Acts of Andrew*. There Andrew tells a demon to leave a young soldier, and it does.[14] What we have in these two stories are cases of exorcism. The apostles recognize the demonic presence, rebuke the demons, and then order them out.

Once again, what we read about reminds us of the gifts of the Spirit. Exorcism is not explicitly mentioned among the Pauline gifts, but the ability to distinguish between spirits is. In addition to this, Irenaeus seems to have thought that it should be classed among the gifts.[15]

The fifth category of spiritual experience is introduced to us in the following passage:

> Some said: "[It is] better for him to die, that he may [not] be in pain." But when Paul had quietened the crowd he [took] his hand, raised him up and asked him, saying: "Hermocrates, [. . .]what thou wilt." But he said: "I wish to eat." (And) he took a loaf and gave him to eat. He became whole in that hour.[16]

The apostle involved meets someone who is sick. In response to his situation, a cure is provided. This, of course, sounds very much like the gift of healing mentioned in 1 Cor 12:9.

The last type of dramatic spiritual ministry I want to point to takes us even further into the realm of the miraculous. In the Apocryphal Acts, there are eleven instances of dead people being restored to life.[17] Involved are men, women, and children of all ages, who have died from a wide variety of causes. It is interesting to see that this sort of miracle appears more frequently in the later Acts than in the earlier ones. For example, the *Acts of John* has many more accounts than the *Acts of Paul*. This should probably be regarded as evidence of the fact that as time passed the Acts became increasingly fabulous in nature and less and less historical.

We note briefly that Paul's lists contain no reference to the raising of the dead, but 1 Cor 12:10 does talk about miracles.

When we look back over this material, we see that the Apocryphal Acts talk about events which remind us of the gifts of the Spirit. They make reference to experiences ranging from discerning of spirits to raising the dead. The authors of these documents were good storytellers. They were out to inspire and to entertain their readers, to fill them with wonder. They must have been very successful. These people had never even dreamed of colored television or moon-walks. Can you imagine the impact that stories about a flying magician, a talking dog, and a lion that asked for Christian baptism must have had? Storytelling—100 percent. Historical accuracy?—0.

Obviously these documents do not tell us much that we can trust about the apostles. However, they do tell us a lot about what these authors and the Christians for whom they wrote could imagine happening. The least we can say is that these Christians had recollections, however vague they might have been, of the gifts of the Spirit.

When you move into Gnosticism and the world of the apocryphal literature, you draw away from the stage where the bishops and the theologians, the well-known figures of the Early Church, played out their roles. You find yourself among the little people, the nameless, faceless masses of Christianity, the "John Does" of the Church. I would really like to get to know them better, but for the most part, they are lost in the shadows. We will probably never know for sure what their lives held, until we meet them in heaven.

However, from what we have looked at here, it seems to me that a frame of mind must have existed among them which would have made it very easy for them to accept the dramatic move of the Spirit through the ministry of the gifts.

Couple this to what we saw in Montanism, Celsus, Irenaeus, and Eusebius, and an interesting picture of the Church in the second half of the second century emerges. These Christians were no strangers to spiritual gifts. They knew that God was still powerfully at work among them, and no doubt they expected to feel the impact of His presence. To a large measure, the Church of these decades continued to be charismatic. The spiritual stream had continued to flow, and it did not stop here.

7

FROM ROME

Several chapters ago I characterized what was happening in the Church of the second half of the second century as sophistication. I commented upon the struggles that were occurring in that period over such matters as organization and doctrine. When we move to the first half of the third century, we discover that the process of sophistication has advanced further. Some of the battles are over, and a greater degree of stability is now to be found in the Church.

It is clear by this time that the structural pattern of bishops, elders, and deacons will prevail over any rivals. Montanism has been dealt with. The Church in the western part of the Roman Empire has weathered the threats of the Marcionites and the Gnostics. These groups will maintain a strong presence in the East for many decades yet, but the West is safe. Many crucial conflicts still lie before the Church, the question of the baptism of heretics and the Arian controversy, to name only two of many, but the Church is established.

Doctrinal upheaval from within and persecution from without will not be able to bring it down. It is well on its way to coming of age when it will occupy the proud position of the dominant religion of the Roman Empire. The "Galilean" will conquer. He has not yet, but He will, and perhaps by this time it could be said that the writing was on the wall. But of course all of this can only be said by means of hindsight.

This period is highly significant for our study. Throughout the

first and second century, Christians enjoyed the presence of the
gifts of the Spirit in their worship. At least that is what the evidence
we have reviewed suggests. However, following about A.D 260
evidence for the presence of spiritual gifts is nonexistent. It looks as
though by then they had ceased to be a part of the day-by-day
experience of the Christians of the time. This means that the block
of time from ca. 200 to 260 is a transitional period as far as the gifts
of the Spirit were concerned.

The Church underwent many changes during the first two and
one-half centuries of its life. Of course there have been other times
of traumatic change, too, but what happened there seems to have
been particularly dramatic. The Christian community grew
phenomenally in size; it became increasingly wealthy; it climbed the
social ladder; its level of education rose; it developed its
organization, and it formalized its worship. While all this was
going on, the gifts of the Spirit just quietly slipped away. Perhaps
no one really noticed it happening. Certainly no one felt concerned
enough to take the trouble to try and stop the trend. The gifts just
disappeared. The crucial time was the early part of the third
century.[1]

The evidence indicates that the gifts were still around. However,
there is no question but that their importance was on the wane and
that attitudes towards them were changing. In this chapter, we will
examine material coming to us from Rome. Two authors there
provide us with relevant information. Interestingly enough, both of
these people spent long periods of their lives outside the Church for
reasons other than their charismatic interests. In fact, one may
have died outside the embrace of mother Church.

Hippolytus

The first of these men is the fiery Hippolytus. He had one of the
best minds in the Church at the time, but he did his writing in
Greek. When the Latin language gained the upper hand among
Roman Christians around the middle of the third century, people
stopped reading his works and he fell into obscurity. However,
there were probably other reasons, too, which prompted readers to
pass him by.

When Callistus became Bishop of Rome ca. 217, Hippolytus split
from him and styled himself Bishop of Rome in opposition. The
issues which divided them seem to have been their beliefs about
Christ and the moral standards which they thought Christians

should live by. In comments he makes about Callistus, Hippolytus shows the sad capacity to hate with a vengeance.[2]

The data which I want us to look at are found in *The Apostolic Tradition,* a document which has traditionally been regarded as Hippolytus' work, and correctly I think. He probably wrote it about A.D. 215, before he defected from the Church. There is every reason to believe that it faithfully reflects what was done in the Roman churches of the late second century. Gregory Dix goes even further saying that much of its content "represents the mind and practice not of St. Hippolytus only but of the whole Catholic Church of the second century."[3] This opinion is probably somewhat stretched, but it is an interesting comment on the importance of the document.

A recent essay by John Stam presents *The Apostolic Tradition* in a light in which it had rarely been placed before.[4] Stam highlights the charismatic nature of the document. He points to the role that the Spirit plays in the ordination of bishops and presbyters, and he draws attention to Spirit-enabled ministry of laymen. These comments of his are valid and appropriate. However, he could have gone further. Specifically, more could have been made of two passages in establishing his basic point.

In passing I would like to note that these two "bolts from the charismatic blue" are somewhat surprising to come across given their contexts. The church which *The Apostolic Tradition* reveals is highly structured. Section 2:1 - 15:1 is given over to a discussion about the clergy. The various levels in the hierarchy are specified, and we are told what the proper method of ordination or appointment to each one is. In 16:1 - 23:14 new members are discussed. It gives details about examinations which are to be given before people are accepted as learners; it makes comments about how long a person should study before being admitted to baptism, and it lays down guidelines for baptism and confirmation. Finally, 24:1 - 38:1 concerns itself with such things as the practice of fasting, the procedure to be followed at the churches' fellowship meals, and the times of prayer. The overriding impression I get from reading this document is that the Christian community that it came from was a closely regulated body. And yet, in spite of this structuring and regimentation, there is evidence that these Christians were familiar with the moving of the Spirit.

The first selection I want us to look at is 15:1—"If anyone among the laity appears to have received a gift of healing by a revelation, hands shall not be laid upon him, because the matter is manifest."[5]

There are a couple of features about this passage which are worth noting. First, it talks about someone's receiving the gift of healing, and it seems fairly clear that what Hippolytus has in mind is probably the same thing that Paul talks about in 1 Cor 12:8 and 28. Secondly, the fact that this gift has been received is announced by "revelation," which appears to be something approximating Paul's "word of knowledge" (1 Cor 12:8). Hippolytus' advice is wise. He says, "Wait and see." If the revelation and the gift of healing were genuine, everyone will know it.

This discussion is very significant for our study. Hippolytus actually seems to have thought that someone might receive a revelation or a gift of healing. The least we can say is he thought this was a definite possibility, otherwise it would have been pointless for him to spend time talking about it. However, perhaps we can go even further. Maybe Hippolytus knew that it was fairly common for people to receive these gifts, and he was just giving some advice to help regulate it all.

The second passage we will go to is 35:3. It reads:

> If a specially gifted teacher should come, let none of you delay to attend the place where the instruction is given, for grace will be given to the speaker to utter things profitable to all, and thou wilt hear new things, and thou wilt be profited by what the Holy Spirit will give thee through the instructor; so thy faith will be strengthened by what thou hearest, and in that place thou wilt learn thy duties at home; therefore let everyone be zealous to go to church, the place where the Spirit abounds.[6]

At first reading, Hippolytus sounds like any other preacher trying to get people to go to church. However, when we look a little closer, we see that a lot more than that is going on. There is charismatic expectancy here.

Note that the speaker's message will be *given* to him. It will come from the Holy Spirit. Secondly, what the teacher says will be "profitable to all." Finally, all of this will happen in the "church," the gathering of believers. The parallel between this and material we find in 1 Corinthians 12 is striking. There we see that God is responsible for the ministry of the gifts, that the gifts will build up everyone, and that it happens when Christians come together. This makes me think that what Hippolytus has in mind is something other than a routine preaching situation. He seems to be describing the ministry of a Christian prophet.[7]

I would also like to underline the way in which Hippolytus speaks of the church. He calls it "the place where the Spirit abounds." Dix points out that the version of *The Apostolic Tradition* in the Sahidic language makes it even stronger. It says the church is the place where the Spirit "breaks forth."[8] At any rate, when Hippolytus went to church, he expected to meet God there, and he anticipated that at least sometimes the divine presence would be shown in dramatic manifestations of the gifts of the Spirit.

The impression these passages leave me with is strong. When I couple it with Stam's observations, my thinking about the churches in Rome of around A.D. 200 is stretched. Not only was it highly structured, but it was also familiar with the gifts of the Spirit.

Novatian

In order to consult the next person who gives us information about the gifts of the Spirit at Rome, we move far into the third century to Novatian. He was a prominent elder in the Christian community, and in fact, on three occasions he was the one who was chosen to write important letters on behalf of all of the elders of the churches in Rome.

However, like Hippolytus, he, too, ran into difficulty with the "establishment." When he was passed over in favor of Cornelius, who became Bishop of Rome in A.D. 251, he had himself consecrated to the same position. This, among other things, led to his being excommunicated in the same year that Cornelius took office. Following this, his personal status among the majority who remained loyal to Cornelius dropped sharply, and very soon afterward the records we have fall silent about him.

However, in spite of this, he continues to occupy a place among the theologians of the Church. This place has been won for him almost single-handedly by one of his books, *Concerning the Trinity*. This study appeared in the A.D 240s and is, in fact, the first major theological work to be written in Latin in Rome. It came out while Novatian was still an eminent, well-respected member of the Roman church.

As the title suggests, *Concerning the Trinity* is about the Trinity, but Novatian by no means devotes equal space to all three members. His discussion of the Holy Spirit seems rather abrupt when you compare it with what he says about the Father and the

Son. Virtually everything relevant to the Spirit is given in chapter 29. We are going to focus upon this chapter because I think it offers some pretty broad hints about the religious experience of Roman Christians in the mid-third century. Specifically, I would suggest that there is information here which may serve as evidence that the spiritual gifts were present in Novatian's church. We will take two steps as we examine this material. First, we will look at what Novatian has to say and then we will study the context in which we find it.

On reading through chapter 29, we find Novatian referring to prophecies about the Holy Spirit from both the Old and New Testaments. He quotes passages from the Gospel of John, chapters 14, 15, and 16, which seems to lead him into a discussion of the significance of the Holy Spirit in the lives of first-generation Christians. This in turn brings him to the spiritual gifts. He says:

> Indeed this is he who appoints prophets in the church, instructs teachers, directs tongues, brings into being powers and conditions of health, carries on extraordinary works, furnishes discernment of spirits, incorporates administrations in the church, establishes plans, brings together and arranges all other gifts there are of the charismata and by reason of this makes the Church of God everywhere perfect in everything and complete.[9]

There are a number of observations about this passage that I would like to make. First, Novatian is talking about "charismatic" gifts. I think it is appropriate to assume that what he is referring to was quite similar to the gifts mentioned by Paul in Romans 12 and 1 Corinthians 12.

Second, he thought they were important. In fact, he puts them in a very elevated position. He says they play a vital role in the perfection and completion of the Church. They are not little trinkets which God has given to people to make them feel good personally. Nor are they embarrassing characteristics of Christians whose emotional stability is questionable. On the contrary, Novatian seems to think that they are essential to the proper development of the Church. I do not think it is stretching things too far to say that Novatian would doubt whether the Church could grow the way God wanted it to without the gifts being active.

Third, and most significant for this study, this passage makes it look as though Novatian was familiar with the gifts of the Spirit. The way in which Novatian speaks of the Spirit is what leads me to think this. He presents Him as the one who *appoints* prophets, *instructs* teachers, *directs* tongues, etc.—all the verbs are in the present tense. Of course these may simply be examples of the "extended present," which does not refer exclusively to the present time. However, we cannot rule out the possibility that Novatian is, in fact, commenting on the church of his time. If he is, this would be evidence of the continuing presence of the gifts of the Spirit among Christians in Rome in the middle part of the third century.

It is obvious that Novatian is influenced by the Apostle Paul in what he says about the spiritual gifts. We can see this clearly by comparing the gifts which Novatian lists to those which appear in 1 Cor 12:8-10 and Rom 12:6-8. Every one of the gifts mentioned by Novatian has a counterpart in one or the other of Paul's lists. Furthermore a Pauline echo may probably be heard in Novatian's "To be sure there are different types of duties in the Spirit,"[10] which is very close to Paul's "There are varieties of gifts . . . service . . . working" (1 Cor 12:4-6). It is fairly clear that through his writings Paul had taught Novatian how to talk about the Spirit's gifts.

In fact, this close contact between the way in which Paul and Novatian talk about the gifts of the Spirit raises a question which is important for us to consider. Is it not possible that Novatian is merely drawing upon a piece of traditional material for the sake of effect? Maybe this passage says nothing at all about what was really going on in the Roman churches. We have to admit that this may be true, but I think the context points us in a different direction. Let us take our second step.

The specific passage we are looking at appears in the part of the 29th chapter of *Concerning the Trinity* in which Novatian is talking about ways in which the Holy Spirit is working.[11] He refers to the spiritual gifts, then leaves the topic to consider the Christian life in general. He says the Holy Spirit is:

> he who brings about the second birth out of waters . . . who may change us into the temple of God and make us his home, who intercedes with divine ears for us with unutterable sighs, fulfilling the duties of an advocate, and displaying the offices of a defender, being given as an inhabitor of our bodies and as one who brings about their holiness.[12]

Novatian thinks that the Holy Spirit is active both at the beginning of an individual's life as a Christian and then throughout it. It seems fairly obvious that he thought the Spirit was doing this in the present. I am sure he would want us to believe that people were receiving the benefits of baptism and being ushered into a relationship with God in his day.

Later in the chapter, he picks up the subject of holiness to which he has just referred and expands what he has said. Approaching the work of the Spirit from a different angle, Novatian observes:

> Indeed this is he who has desires contrary to the flesh, because the flesh fights against him. This is he who restrains unsatiable, passionate longing, breaks unbridled lust, puts out illicit ardour, conquers flagrant impulses, flings aside drunkenness, banishes greed, avoids dissolute revellings . . . turns out the impure.[13]

It seems that Novatian has seen a higher degree of moral behavior in Christians than in non-Christians, and he thinks the explanation for this is to be found in the work of the Holy Spirit. But not only does the Spirit improve morality, He also "binds together affections" and "draws together good-will."[14] In other words, He builds relationships among people.

Looking in another direction, we see Novatian focusing on doctrinal matters. He was living at a time when many Christians were arriving at a consensus of opinion with each other on doctrine. In the process of doctrinal consolidation, Novatian sees the handiwork of the Spirit. He tells us that the Spirit "repels sects, prepares the rule of truth, refutes heretics,"[15] and "keeps the Church pure and inviolate by the sanctity of uninterrupted virginity and of truth."[16] So in this area, too, the Holy Spirit is at work.

As we review *Concerning the Trinity,* 29, it appears that Novatian thought the Spirit was very active in his day. He is not concerned in the first instance with what had happened at some earlier time in history; he is relating what is occurring at his time.

So now we can bring our discussion of Novatian to a conclusion. In the 29th chapter of *Concerning the Trinity,* he points to various areas in which he thinks the Holy Spirit is working. He makes reference to doctrinal unity, holiness, prayer, baptism, and spiritual gifts. There is no discernible difference in the manner in which he talks about what the Spirit does in these areas. He says that what is going on in all of them can be explained in terms of the working of the Spirit. If we can grant that any of these things were going on in the Church of Novatian's time, we have grounds for assuming that they were all there. It is certain that people were being baptized and that Christians were moving towards doctrinal uniformity. Also there were probably people around whose moral lives had improved as a result of their becoming Christians. Therefore, it is more than possible that the spiritual gifts were to be found in Novatian's church, too, and that we can say that *Concerning the Trinity,* 29, offers evidence that the gifts of the Spirit were still to be found among Christians in Rome around A.D. 250.

The picture which comes together of mid-third century Christianity in Rome is an intriguing one. Believers there worshipped in a fairly tightly organized community under the direction of a clearly defined hierarchy. Many steps had been taken to regularize their Christian lives. The great and powerful Roman Catholic Church was looming on the horizon. In the midst of all this growth of form and structure, we come across evidence which points to the conclusion that spontaneous worship was still around. These Christians were probably quite familiar with the ministry of the spiritual gifts, and Rome was not the only place where this was true either.

8

FROM CARTHAGE

As we press on with our study of the gifts of the Spirit in the early third century Church, we shift our attention away from Rome and across the Mediterranean Sea to its ancient rival. We must listen to the voices of two Carthaginians. These men occupy very different places in the history of the Church. The relationship of one with Mother Church has remained uneasy from his day to ours, while the other one coined the famous phrase, "One cannot have God as Father without having the Church as Mother." I am referring, of course, to Tertullian and Cyprian.

Their writings give us an extremely vivid picture of life among Christians in North Africa in the early third century. As we read, we are caught up in the struggles, tensions, victories, defeats, heroism, and cowardice, which mark their works. What unfolds before us is high drama.

This literature also sheds light on the spirituality of these two men and their contemporaries. We find references to what was happening in the devotional lives not only of the great and well-known, but also the nameless, "average" Christian.

One conclusion to which we are led has to do with the gifts of the Spirit. The Church of this period and area was no stranger to the dramatic moving of the Spirit. Both Tertullian and Cyprian provide us with information which is relevant. Let us start with Tertullian.

Tertullian

When we turn to Tertullian, we are looking at "l'enfant terrible" of the Early Church. In an age in which many Christian authors expressed themselves with deep passion, bias, and severity, Tertullian tops the heap. His work fairly bristles with irony, sarcasm, and ridicule. He writes with intensity like a killer shark hunts its prey!

As devastating as he is in debate, his work also sparkles with doctrinal brilliance (it took the rest of the Church a century or more to catch up with his thinking). He coins expressions as he goes along, such as "trinity," creating a theological vocabulary which we are still using today. He seems to come up with adequate ways of talking about the Trinity and the natures of Christ with relatively little effort.

Tertullian stands (larger than life) out of his writings, in spite of the fact that we know very few of the details of his life. Most of what we thought we knew on the basis of what Jerome says about him in his book, *Concerning Famous Men,* has been overthrown by T. D. Barnes.[1]

However, there are a couple of important comments which we can make. We know that he actively wrote for 20 years, beginning about A.D. 197. We also know that part way through his career he encountered the Montanists. From about A.D. 207 on we find an increasing number of references to the early leaders of Montanism, Montanus, Maximilla, and Priscilla, and we find Tertullian borrowing Montanist vocabulary. Nevertheless, I think that there are many factors which suggest that we had better be careful about assuming Tertullian gave himself unreservedly to the Montanists in 207, or any other date for that matter.[2] But we cannot go into that here.

With these comments about Tertullian's life behind us, we can move on to his writings. His work contains more references and allusions to the gifts of the Spirit than we can find in what has survived from any other early Christian author. He also has a greater feeling for the gifts than do many other authors who talk about them. In fact, we find the gifts mentioned in six different places in Tertullian.

The first of these that we will look at comes from his five-volume work, *Against Marcion.* Here Tertullian has trained his guns on an arch-enemy of the Church, and he is blasting away, using arguments that at times become extremely involved.

Without carrying us too far from the main subject of this study, we should pause over Marcion's teaching. Among other things, he believed that there were two gods; the good supreme god, who revealed himself through Jesus and of whom Paul was a faithful apostle, and the evil creator god, who is revealed in the Old Testament. Tertullian absolutely rejects this whole idea.

In book 5 of this work, he sets out to show that the God whom Paul served was, in fact, none other than the Creator, the God of the Old Testament. In order to do so, he draws material from Paul's epistles. In doing this, he is moving onto Marcion's ground, because Marcion's "Bible" was made up of only a carefully edited Gospel of Luke and 10 of Paul's epistles.

Eventually, in book 5, chapter 8, Tertullian turns to that section of 1 Corinthians which talks about the gifts of the Spirit, and here he thinks he has the means by which he can scuttle Marcion once for all. We are prepared for decisive combat. At one end of the lists Marcion, who accepts what Paul says about the gifts, fidgets nervously upon his charger. At the other, waits Tertullian, calm in the conviction that what Paul has to say about spiritual gifts is in fulfillment of Old Testament prophecy. When the scarf is dropped, who will come out victorious? As far as Tertullian is concerned, the answer is simple: the one who can produce the gifts.

Tertullian hurls out a challenge, "So then let Marcion put in evidence any gifts there are of his god."[3] He wants to hear a true prophecy, a psalm, an ecstatic prayer, an interpretation of tongues, or maybe he could be told about a vision. These he would regard as proofs of Marcion's position.

He goes on to say, "If all such proofs are more readily put in evidence by me . . . the apostle will belong to my God." And there he rests his case. The point I want to emphasize is simple: Tertullian's whole argument would fall to the ground if the gifts of the Spirit were not to be found among the Christian group he belonged to. If they were not there, he would be throwing caution to the wind by bluffing wildly, and he would be tremendously embarrassed if anyone called his bluff. I cannot imagine Tertullian putting himself in that position. I think that this is strong evidence that some Carthaginian Christians were very familiar with the ministry of spiritual gifts.

This same impression is gained from the second passage from Tertullian's work which we will look at. In his essay entitled

Concerning the Soul, he is attempting a careful discussion of that part of man. He points out that, unlike secular philosophers, what he can learn about the soul is not confined only to reason. What he has learned this way has been supplemented by information gained through revelation. He claims that his group had merited the gift of prophecy, through which a woman had given him many insights into the nature of the human soul.[4]

What interests me is not this claim to prophecy, although that is significant in itself. I am more concerned with the grounds upon which Tertullian thinks his community had become eligible to prophesy. He says that it had happened because "we acknowledge the spiritual gifts."[5] Prophecy could occur because they believed that spiritual gifts were important and that they were in the Church. A little later he implies that no one should be surprised at this, because this is exactly the way the Apostle Paul had said it would be.[6]

Once again Tertullian and the Christians he belonged to come forward as people who placed a lot of value on the gifts of the Spirit.

The third passage is very similar to the one we have just looked at. The same claim is made, in quite a different context, and it has the same impact. In the process of introducing a discussion of his view of marriage, Tertullian characterizes himself and his friends as those whose "recognition of the spiritual gifts makes it correct (for them) to be called spiritual."[7] Again, the statement that they value the gifts of the Spirit is what is of chief importance.

Fourthly, we take up a passage from the *Passion (or Martyrdom) of Perpetua and Felicitas.* These two young women died heroically for their faith at Carthage in A.D. 202. It seems likely that Tertullian was the editor of this work and that he authored several of its chapters.[8]

The material we are interested in is found very near the beginning. We read:

> We recognize and honor the prophecies and the recent visions which had been promised equally. We also regard the rest of the powers of the Holy Spirit as tools of the Church to whom the Spirit was sent, administering all of the outstandingly impressive gifts to everyone just as the Lord distributes to each.[9]

There are several points arising from this that I want to call attention to. First, note that Tertullian equates prophecy and the recent visions. The first expression most likely refers to Old Testament prophecy, while the second should probably be understood as what has come from the Montanists. If this is true, Tertullian has placed them on an equal footing. All of this suggests that Tertullian was prepared to award very high status to the oracles of Montanus, Maximilla, and Priscilla.

Secondly, we observe that both the Spirit and the Lord are said to parcel out the gifts. This parallels what we find in 1 Cor 12:4-6. In both passages, more than one divine person is associated with the gifts.

Thirdly, it is interesting to pause over the word which I have translated "outstandingly impressive gifts." It is *donativum,* and it is used elsewhere to mean a gift given by an emperor. It suggests rich, even lavish presents with nothing common about them. Tertullian had great appreciation for what the Spirit was giving to the Church.

The last passage from Tertullian's works which we will consider is *Concerning Baptism,* 20:5:

> Therefore, blessed ones whom the grace of God awaits, when you come up out of that most holy bath which brings about new birth and for the first time raise your hands within your Mother, the Church, with your brothers, ask the Father, ask the Lord to make you subject to the riches of grace, the distribution of the gifts.[10]

The phrase to be noted particularly is "the distribution of the gifts." In the light of what we have seen of Tertullian's thinking about the gifts elsewhere, it is pretty certain that he has the gifts of the Spirt in mind here. If that is so, Tertullian is encouraging newly baptized members of the Church to ask for spiritual gifts and to expect to receive them. He seems to regard this as normal Christian experience.

Having looked carefully at several passages from Tertullian's writings, we can draw some conclusions about the place which the Spirit's gifts occupied both in the life and thought of Tertullian, himself, and in the experience of other Carthaginian Christians.

First, it is illuminating to think about the dates when the works which carry references to the gifts of the Spirit were written. *Concerning Baptism* and *The Martyrdom of Perpetua and Felicitas* appeared early in Tertullian's career, *Against Marcion* and *Concerning the Soul* came just after half-way, and *Concerning Monogamy,* near the end. The deduction I want to make from this is fairly simple. The gifts of the Spirit were not passing fancies with Tertullian, nor were they novelties that cropped up late in his life. He knew them throughout his literary career, and his high regard for them never slipped.

All of this has provided us with some intriguing insights into Carthaginian Christianity in general. Tertullian states that newly baptized Christians should expect to receive the gifts of the Spirit in church (*Concerning Baptism,* 20, 5), and he speaks of the gifts with warm approval (*Martyrdom of Perpetua and Felicitas,* 1). Furthermore, twice he states plainly the Christian group he belongs to acknowledges spiritual gifts as valid (*Concerning the Soul,* 9, 3 and *Concerning Monogamy,* 1, 2), and once he implies very strongly that the gifts can be found with ease within the part of the Church that he belongs to (*Against Marcion,* 5, 8:12).

The really significant point is that between the times when he wrote the first two works mentioned and when he published the last three he is supposed to have undergone a change in loyalties—to have abandoned the Catholics in favor of the Montanists. However, it is evident that there is very little change in his thinking about the gifts of the Spirit. Does this mean that both the Catholics and the Montanists in early third-century Carthage were well-acquainted with the gifts? If in fact Tertullian did switch from one group to the other, I think the answer is yes. However, there are some other possibilities. Maybe these two groups were not as far apart as we normally think they were. Maybe the split in the Carthaginian church was not as deep as it first appears.

Cyprian

Leaving Tertullian, we turn attention to the famous Bishop, Cyprian. The lives of these two men may have overlapped by a decade or so, and there is no question but that Tertullian's theology influenced Cyprian. Nonetheless, there are real differences between the roles the two men played in their church. Both found themselves in the eye of storms repeatedly, but Tertullian was there stirring up problems, while Cyprian was usually trying to defuse explosive situations and control things.

Prior to becoming a Christian, Cyprian seems to have carved out a secure place for himself in Carthage. Apparently he taught rhetoric and owned a fair amount of property.

He seems to have become a Christian about A.D. 245, and within 4 years he was at the head of the church in Carthage as bishop. For a decade he guided his church through one agonizing upheaval after another. Finally, he sealed his efforts with his blood. He was beheaded for his faith in A.D. 258.

Cyprian is best known for his thinking about the Church and the place of the bishop in it. His ideas on these subjects have been influential right up to the present. However, they were not hatched after long incubation. Quite to the contrary, they took shape during a time of seething controversy. Cyprian found himself forced to think out positions on such thorny problems as what to do with those who had denied Christ during persecution and how to handle those who had been baptized by heretics and who now wanted to join the Catholic Church. Much of his thinking played an essential role in shaping Catholic theory regarding the Church.

In the light of this, I find it fascinating that Cyprian was "also among the prophets." Here is a man perched on the highest rung of church government, a powerful bishop. He was call "Papa" (pope) just like the Bishop of Rome and a few others were, and yet, he held a very lively interest in direct intervention by God in human affairs through the gifts of the Spirit. He found room for spontaneous responses to God in the midst of his demanding life at the head of an important diocese. A number of modern scholars have seen this aspect of Cyprian,[11] but no one has highlighted it better than Adolf von Harnack. In a very conclusive manner, he marshalled evidence in support of the claim that Cyprian was very concerned about things related to the Spirit.[12]

Interestingly enough, the great Carthaginian bishop does not seem to have been the only one in North Africa who was familiar with dramatic moves of God. His writings indicate that there were others also who were experiencing much the same things as he was. Let us look at several passages from those writings.

First, we will focus on Cyprian himself. Not only have modern students of history seen him as a prophet, but so did his contemporaries. This comes out in a letter written to Cyprian from several Christians who were suffering under the Valerian persecution. In this letter, they say:

> For by your words you have both provided those things about which we have been taught the least and strengthened us to bear up under the sufferings which we are experiencing, being certain of the heavenly reward, the martyrs' crown, and the kingdom of God as a result of the prophecy which you, being full of the Holy Spirit pledged to us in your letter.[13]

Rightly or wrongly, these Christians thought that what Cyprian had written to them was prophecy.

Harnack argues that Cyprian would have agreed with them, at least in some cases. He says that when Cyprian states that one of his essays, *The Benefit of Patience,* was written with help given "by the Lord, who permits and inspires," he was claiming that his words had been authorized by Christ.[14]

Secondly, let me point out that Cyprian sometimes referred to special spiritual experiences he had had in order to lend weight to his words. *Letter 66* illustrates this. There he is defending himself from the attack of Florentius Pupianus. Apparently Florentius had been questioning Cyprian's place in the Catholic Church. In response to this, Cyprian—in a style which at times is bitingly sarcastic—presents several factors which support his contention that he is a worthy bishop of the Church. He warns Florentius to repent and to attempt to patch up their relationship. Then, as if to give his words greater punch, he says:

> In fact I remember what has already been shown to me, indeed what has been taught to an obedient and fearing servant by the Lord God, who thought it worthwhile to show and reveal these among other things and who adds this, "Therefore he who does not believe Christ who makes the priest, shall later begin to believe him who avenges the priest." And yet, I know that to some men dreams are seen to be ridiculous and visions silly, but certainly more so to those who choose to think badly of the priests than to those who are favorable to them.[15]

Here, in order to buttress his argument, Cyprian calls upon a message which he claims was given to him by God through a special revelation.

There is no doubt but that Cyprian thought that what had happened to him was valid. However, the last sentence in the passage points out that not everyone agreed with him. He has to admit that some think that dreams "are ridiculous" and "visions silly." Attitudes towards spiritual manifestations were changing. Up to this point, what we have read about the gifts in early Christian literature has been favorable. The Church reacted strongly to the Montanist movement, but even there we do not come across anything which suggests that the gifts themselves were being questioned. Here we do. There were now skeptics in the Church. Indeed, times had changed.

The next relevant piece of material we can turn to comes from

Cyprian's essay, *Concerning Mortality*. There certainly were skeptics among North African Christians, but at the same time, there were others in addition to Cyprian who were enjoying dramatic encounters with God. The passage we are going on to helps us to see that.

Concerning Mortality was written following the onslaught of a plague which brought the people of Carthage into daily contact with death. This situation threw some Christians into confusion, and Cyprian wrote, trying to provide a Christian interpretation of the event. At one point he states that it is not appropriate for a Christian to struggle, to complain, and to seek to escape when confronted by death. In supporting this idea, Cyprian calls upon the experience of another African bishop.

This man was at the point of death and was praying that his life might be prolonged when:

> There stood by . . . a young man, venerable in grace and dignity, lofty in stature, and brilliant in appearance and upon whom, as he stood by human sight was scarcely able to gaze with its fleshly eyes.[16]

This ethereal youth then spoke to the bishop and expressed disapproval with his hesitation to die. Cyprian then goes on:

> Our dying brother and colleague heard what he might say to others. For he heard it while he was dying, he heard it so that he might tell it: he heard it not for himself, but for us.[17]

Here was a man, as Cyprian's comment shows, who had been given a message by God which he was to convey to others. He comes close to being a prophet.

The passion, heat, and confusion of a period of intense persecution early in Cyprian's time as bishop are the circumstances out of which further evidence of prophetic activity in North Africa arises. Upon the outbreak of the Decian persecution, Cyprian went into hiding. Although he kept up correspondence with the clergy of his church, he soon began to lose control of what was happening there. He learned that some of the elders had started to let people who had offered sacrifices in order to avoid persecution come back into the church. This was in flat disobedience to Cyprian's instructions. He writes, saying that these elders have been wrong to do what they have, and then, before he orders that the practice be stopped, he says:

> Because of this the divine judgment does not stop restraining us night

or day. In addition to visions in the night, during the day also among us the innocent age of childhood is filled with the Holy Spirit. It sees with its eyes in ecstasy, it hears, and it speaks those things of which the Lord thinks it is worthwhile to warn and to instruct us.[18]

Here Cyprian refers to prophetic messages which he was hearing while in hiding and which were relevant to the subject he was discussing. The agents of these messages appear to have been children.

From all of these passages, we conclude that North Africa was not foreign to the gifts of the Spirit around the mid-point of the third century. The most important bishop of the area, Cyprian, had experienced the moving of God's Spirit, as had at least one other bishop. In addition to that, a number of children in Cyprian's place of hiding had been involved with the same sort of thing. In spite of questions which were arising, Carthaginian Christianity continued to have a charismatic element in it.

We can now draw our conclusion about the early third century North African church and the gifts of the Spirit. First, I think we have to say that the atmosphere was charismatic. What we have dug out of Tertullian and Cyprian suggests pretty strongly that Christians in this time and place were certainly not strangers to the movings of the Spirit. I find it enlightening to compare the ways in which these two men discuss the gifts. Tertullian certainly gives them more space, but they generally talk about the same kind of experiences. They make reference only to gifts which give information about God and His will, referring to visions, revelations, and prophecies.

In addition to this, let us note that these Carthaginian Christian leaders held fairly similar ideas about what prophecy was like. They both make reference to occasions when people had visions or received revelations from God, which they later shared with others. This lacks some of the directness which seems to be assumed in 1 Corinthians 12, but it fits quite well with what we find in Acts 10 and Acts 16, where Peter and Paul had visions, and also with some material in Acts 21 related to the ministry of the prophet Agabus.

And so the gifts of the Spirit were still around. Whether people were Montanist or Catholic does not seem to have mattered much. As in Rome, at least some North African Christians were involved in ministry through the gifts of the Spirit.

However, we also have to note that these same gifts had their detractors. People were raising questions about them. Attitudes towards them were changing. As we now shift attention to another region, we will see much the same picture develop.

9

FROM THE GREEK EAST

Up to now, our discussion of the gifts of the Spirit in the third century Church has kept us around the west end of the Mediterranean. With the exception of Hippolytus, we have been dealing with leaders of Latin-speaking Christianity. In this chapter we move to the other end of the Roman Empire. More specifically, all the material we will be looking at comes from a Greek Christian circle of intellectuals dominated by Origen.

In terms of its development, the Greek Church of this period was pretty much on a par with its Latin counterpart. Its organization was advanced, centering around powerful bishops. Its people had experienced the same economic and social improvement that we noted in the West. However, it may even have been a step ahead of the West in that it had theological schools which were able to claim attention not only from Christians but also from pagans. And of course, the outstanding Christian teacher of the time was Origen. There were other significant ones, too, Clement and Heraclas, for example, but Origen outshone them all.

As we attempt to review evidence related to the gifts, we will consult Origen and two of his pupils who went on to become powerful bishops, Dionysius of Alexandria and Firmilian. Let us turn to the "master" first.

Origen

Origen is an outstanding figure in the history of the Church and one of its greatest minds. He studied philosophy, taught an incredibly wide range of theological material, and practiced a rigidly devout Christian life. In addition to his devotional and intellectual achievements, he was a committed churchman. Frequently we find him on the road to somewhere in order to defend the true doctrine of the Church.

Unfortunately, not everything about Origen is rosy. On one hand, his devotion had the taint of fanaticism. On the other hand, his philosophy seems to have corrupted his theology. Almost 300 years after his death, the Church officially condemned many of his ideas.

We approach Origen here simply because a number of his works contain references to the gifts of the Spirit. As we consider these passages, we will do well to keep in mind a comment made by Jean Daniélou. While he was discussing what Origen's works had to say about certain matters related to the Church, he suggested that:

> With reference to each of these points we shall have to consider on the one hand the evidence Origen provides about the concrete facts as they were in his time, and on the other his own personal view of them.[1]

If we hold onto this distinction, I think it will help to clarify statements Origen makes about the spiritual gifts. We will take two steps as we examine these statements. First, we will listen to what Origen has to say, and then, we will attempt to assess its significance.

As I mentioned a moment ago, the gifts of the Spirit crop up fairly frequently in Origen's writings. He never lays out a complete theology of the gifts, but sometimes we can pick up hints about how he thought they worked in day-to-day experience. At other points, he reports on their presence in the Church of his time. Taking Daniélou's advice, we will look first at one type of material and then the other.

When we examine Origen's thinking about the contemporary role of the gifts, we find him mentioning two much more frequently than the others. These are the "word of wisdom" and the "word of knowledge." He refers to them in *First Principles,* 1, 3:8 and 2, 7:3; in *Against Celsus,* 3, 18; 3, 46, and 7, 23, and in *On Joshua,* 8:1 and 26:2. He also talks about prophecy in *On Exodus,* 4, 5. He thinks these gifts fulfill a very specific function. They are given to help people who interpret Scripture. When you are doing this, you frequently come up against passages that are hard to understand. The thing to do then, he says, is to pray for one of the gifts we have just mentioned. If it is given, your chances of interpreting the passage well will be much better, because God will be helping you. The gifts are Bible study aids.

Origen also thought that the gifts of the Spirit had another role to play in the Church. As he saw it, perhaps the main purpose of the gifts was to bring personal benefit to individual Christians. This comes out very clearly in *Against Celsus,* 3, 18. There he says that the word of wisdom and the word of knowledge help students to learn and really understand the Christian faith. Once again, the gifts are presented as study aids, but this time it is the one who is studying who gets the help, whereas in the other passages we have just cited, it is the teacher.

This way of thinking about the gifts fits well with Origen's general theological outlook. To a large degree, he saw the Christian life as the pursuit of true knowledge. In addition to this, when he set about interpreting Scripture, he was by no means content to rest with the surface, or literal, or historical-grammatical meaning. He was constantly searching for the deep "spiritual" meaning. In order to perceive that, and in order to arrive at true knowledge, the gifts were essential as far as he was concerned.

Origen's idea of the gifts certainly corresponded well to the rest of his theological system. However, his understanding of them was a long way from the Apostle Paul. Paul saw them as functioning in the Christian community, for the benefit of that community as a whole. They were not given to strengthen individuals' intellectual grasp on Christianity.

Having looked at Origen's thinking about the contemporary functioning of the gifts, we can now move on to the reports he gives about them. He saw them in the Church around him, and he makes some important comments. There are four passages in which we find reports, and they all come from his *Against Celsus.* Each of them expresses the idea that "traces" of the gifts of the Holy Spirit remain among Christians. We will look at these passages together and make some detailed comments on them later.

Against Celsus, 1, 2.

Here Origen is talking about how you can show that the Gospel is valid. As he does so, he states that the miracles which testified to the truth of the Gospel in the Apostolic age are proved to have happened by the fact that traces of them still exist. He says:

> This more divine demonstration the apostle calls a "demonstration of spirit and of power"—of spirit because of the prophecies and especially those which refer to Christ, which are capable of convincing anyone who reads them; of power because of the prodigious miracles which may be proved to have happened by this argument among many others, that traces of them still remain among those who live according to the will of the Logos.[2]

Against Celsus, 1, 46.

In this passage, once he has talked about miracles as we see them in Jesus' ministry and then as they appeared in the Early Church, Origen goes on to say:

> Traces of that Holy Spirit who appeared in the form of a dove are still preserved among Christians. They charm demons away and perform many cures and perceive certain things about the future according to the will of the Logos.[3]

Against Celsus, 2, 8.

Origen is here discussing the lot of the Jews since the birth of Jesus.

> They no longer have any prophets or wonders, though traces of these are to be found to a considerable extent among Christians. Indeed, some works are even greater; and if our word may be trusted, we also have seen them.[4]

Against Celsus, 7, 8.

In this passage, Origen is considering a claim made by Celsus that he had seen prophets in Palestine.

> But signs of the Holy Spirit were manifested at the beginning when Jesus was teaching, and after his ascension there were many more, though later they became less numerous. Nevertheless, even to this day there are traces of him in a few people whose souls have been purified by the Logos and by the actions which follow his teaching.[5]

There are several points arising out of these passages which I would like us to look at a little more closely. First, let us try to find out what these "traces" to which Origen referred were. In 1, 2, miracles are mentioned; in 2, 8, prophets and wonders, and in 7, 8, signs of the Holy Spirit. However, in 1, 46 Origen gets a little more specific, listing three "traces," and what he says parallels the lists of gifts given in Romans 12 and 1 Corinthians 12 in several ways. In both Origen's and Paul's lists there are references to the action which people are enabled to take towards good and bad spirits. In Origen's statement, Christians charm out bad spirits, while Paul mentions the ability to distinguish among spirits. In addition to this, both talk about the ability to heal the sick. Furthermore, the ability to foresee the future, mentioned by Origen, squares well with one aspect of the New Testament prophet's ministry as we see it in the life of Agabus (Acts 21:11). In 1 Corinthians, we are told God is responsible for the appearance of the gifts, while in *Against Celsus*, 1, 46 the same sort of thing is regarded as a sign of the work of the Holy Spirit. I think that all these points of contact mean that Origen's "traces" were the same things as Paul's "gifts." As far as I can see, this carries over to the other passages from Origen's *Against Celsus* too.

However, did we not just say a couple of pages ago that Origen's thinking about the gifts differed from Paul's? Yes. But let us notice a further distinction. When we were looking at Origen's thinking about the gifts, we found him mentioning three in particular, "the word of wisdom," "the word of knowledge," and "prophecy." All three are viewed as means by which God gives us more information about Himself.

The reports, on the other hand, go quite a ways beyond this. The reports mention prophecy, but the other gifts by which revelations about God are given do not appear. Rather, we hear about "miracles," "healing," "exorcism," and "wonders." Origen's thinking about the "revelation" gifts does not make it impossible for us to assume a similarity between other gifts he mentions and the gifts in the New Testament. With regard to these, Origen was simply "calling it as he saw it."

There is a second fact emerging from these passages to which we must give full weight. Origen says repeatedly that it is only "traces" of the Spirit and of the Spirit's work which remain. Furthermore, in *Against Celsus*, 7, 8, he tells us that the traces of the Spirit are observable "in a few people." It is obvious that by the time Origen wrote this book—the mid-third century—the tide of charismatic experience within the Church had ebbed considerably. Origen knew that the gifts had once been common features in the life of the Church, but, by the time he had reached the later part of his life, their appearance had ceased to be common.

A third point which we should pause over arises from *Against*

Celsus, 2, 8. This passage contains a phrase which is a bit confusing. We have just seen that Origen thought that the gifts were rather unusual by his time. However, now we find him coming out with something quite different. His comment is that although prophecy and wonders have disappeared from the Jews, there are still traces of them among Christians and this (here is the surprising phrase) "to a considerable extent." And furthermore, once he has made the proper and polite qualifications, "and if our word may be trusted," Origen proceeds to claim that he had actually seen the gifts with his own eyes. How are we to make sense of this change of direction? Is this just window dressing to improve the Church's image? We will answer those questions, but first let us spend a little more time thinking about Origen as a man.

First of all, we have to see Origen as a man of the Church. I mentioned this earlier, but we should give it more attention. Throughout his life he served the Church with great devotion. Daniélou stresses this point, saying:

> We have seen from his life that he had been catechist, lector, priest, doctor, and martyr by turns: the whole of his life was spent in the discharge of ecclesiastical functions. In that respect, his works are deeply rooted in the Christianity of his time.[6]

Origen was a person who simply had to "be about his Church's business."

Not only was this true, but he was highly regarded by his fellow Christians, and of course these two observations go hand in hand with each other. He may have fallen out of favor with the Church after his death, but he rode the crest of a wave of popularity during his life.

While living at Alexandria, his highly disciplined life and vast intellectual gifts won him widespread fame. He was "All-Mediterranean" in both philosophical thinking and philosophical living. In fact, he won honors in every league he was ever in. His reputation was so good that even his excommunication by Bishop Demetrius of Alexandria and his subsequent move to Caesarea could only tarnish it slightly.

Among other things, Origen served his Church as a kind of theological "trouble-shooter." On at least two occasions, he was called in to assist in peace negotiations in the Middle East—theological peace, of course. Eusebius tells us that on each occasion he played a prominent role.

We have to remember, too, that Origen travelled on other than peace-keeping missions also. He lived and taught in Alexandria and Caesarea, but he also visited Rome, Arabia, Antioch, Greece, and another Caesarea (in Cappadocia) for various reasons. A globetrotter like this must have had a pretty comprehensive outlook on Christianity. He had not wrapped himself in his blanket and huddled by the home fire. He had gotten out and seen a large part of the world. I can imagine him visiting with Christians in many different places. I am sure they sat up far into the night, cup or glass of whatever in hand, solving all the problems of the Church and the world of their day, in the same way we do. My guess is that these sessions really helped Origen to find the pulse of contemporary Christianity.

Taking our sketch of Origen a step further, I would just like to emphasize that Origen was no wild-eyed charismatic trying to build a case for his gifts. In fact, as we saw earlier, he held an understanding of spiritual gifts which I think is even more conservative than the moderate view which Paul held. The reports of the gifts, and of course it is these which are most important for our study, do not come out of a fervent defense of the gifts. They pop up almost incidentally in passages where the main subject is something else.

All of this suggests to me that Origen was in a good position from which to comment on the spiritual life of the Church. Furthermore, I think we can assume that when Origen speaks about the gifts of the Spirit, he will be fairly unbiased.

So what do we conclude? Well, Origen says he has seen "traces" of the gifts of the Spirit. I think this means that in Origen's time the gifts occasionally appeared. Where? Who knows for sure? Maybe in only one or two places, or maybe throughout a wide area of the Empire. Origen does not tell us where he had found them. However, there were only "traces." By Origen's time the gifts were pretty clearly well along on their way out of the Early Church. At this point we leave one of the most original thinkers the Church has ever known.

Dionysius

We move now to Dionysius, one of Origen's more famous pupils. The heady atmosphere that surrounded the teacher certainly marked the pupil, because he went on to establish a reputation for learning in his own right. However, unlike Origen, Dionysius climbed to the top of ecclesiastical power when he became Bishop of Alexandria in A.D. 247. He held that position for 17 very difficult years, guiding his ship with a firm hand through the heavy waters of doctrinal controversy, persecution, civil disorder, and plague.

Dionysius, however, seems to have controlled his power, rather than the other way around; the way it often is. He is one of the nicest people I have met in the Early Church. He consistently comes over as a man capable of approaching difficult situations reasonably and coolly. He was always prepared to listen to the other fellow and to try to find a way to work things out without hurting somebody. However, he was not so broad-minded that he was flat! He had a pretty clear idea of what Truth was, and he worked hard to preserve it. But he always tried to do it with love. Unfortunately, this kind of person is rare in any period of Church history.

It is encouraging to find that as deeply immersed as Dionysius was in theology and in governing his church, he also had an appreciation for direct contact with God. I would like to point to a couple of incidents that illustrate this and then make a brief comment on them.

The incidents I refer to come from two very important moments in Dionysius' life. The first appeared in the midst of persecution. Shortly after Decius had begun his attack on the Church, it was learned that Dionysius was no longer in Alexandria. The captain of the troops had "turned tail" and fled! Later Dionysius had to write defending himself against charges of cowardice. There is one very interesting phrase embedded in his explanation. He says, "God bade me depart."[7] He claims to have acted on direct orders from God.

The second event is very similar to the one we have just looked at. We find Dionysius locked in the middle of the controversy swirling around people who had been baptized by heretics and who now wanted to join the Church. Characteristically, Dionysius was trying to reach the best, fairest decision possible. He was wrestling with the problem of whether or not to read the actual writings of the heretics. His natural inclinations told him to do so, but he thought he would be running the risk of theological pollution if he took them up. What should he do? In the midst of his confusion, God spoke. Let Dionysius tell us.

> But a vision sent by God came and strengthened me, and a word of command was given me, saying expressly: "Read all things that may

come to thy hand. For thou art able to sift and prove each matter; which thing was originally the cause of thy faith.'' I accepted the vision.[8]

Dionysius does not look like the obstinate bishop here, but he certainly does come off as a man who wanted to hear from God.

How do we assess this material? We probably cannot insist that what Dionysius experienced conforms closely to what we read about in 1 Corinthians 12. As I have suggested several times, the gifts we meet in the Pauline material were given for the good of the whole assembly of believers, and they usually appeared in meetings of the group. Dionysius is getting direct personal guidance in much the same way that Paul did before striking off into Macedonia. I think the most we can say is that the kind of openness to God which we see in the New Testament persists in Dionysius. However, the evidence we have from him says very little, if anything, about the actual gifts of the Spirit.

Firmilian

The last individual we will consult is Firmilian, Bishop of Caesarea in Cappadocia, now eastern Turkey. He has a lot in common with Dionysius of Alexandria. Both studied with Origen, both became bishops, both served in the A.D. 250s and 260s, and both became deeply involved in the same doctrinal struggles. However, the characters of the two men differed greatly. Firmilian was as harsh and sarcastic as Dionysius was peace-loving and gentle. It would be interesting to see these two men discussing something around a board room table.

In A.D. 256 Firmilian wrote Cyprian a rather long letter, and it has survived among the Bishop of Carthage's correspondence. There is one passage in it which I would like to quote at length.

About twenty-two years ago, . . . suddenly there arose here a certain woman who in a state of ecstasy put herself forward as a prophetess and acted as if she were filled with the Holy Spirit. But, on the contrary, she was being carried by the force of the chief demons in such a way that for a long time she disturbed and deceived the church, bringing about certain astonishing and extraordinary things, and she also promised that she would move the earth. (Not that the power of the demon was so great that he was strong enough to move the earth or disturb the elements, but that sometimes an evil spirit, knowing in advance that there would be an earthquake, pretends that he will do what he sees happening in the future.) With these lies and boasts he had subdued the minds of many so that they were obedient to him and followed wherever he advised or led. He also made that woman walk bare-footed through frozen snow in the dead of winter and prevented her from being troubled by it or being injured by the walk. Also she would say that she was hurrying to Judea and Jerusalem, feigning as if she had come from there. Here also she led astray a presbyter, a man with a rural background, and another deacon also, in order that they might join the woman—which was discovered soon afterwards. Suddenly one of the exorcists confronted her, a man who had been proven and who always lived a religiously disciplined life, who, also inspired by the exhortation of many brethren who were present, who even themselves were strong and praiseworthy in the faith, rose up to subdue that evil spirit, which also had a short time earlier, with subtle deceit, predicted that a certain opposing and unbelieving assailant would come. However, the exorcist inspired by the grace of God resisted strongly and showed that spirit which was previously thought to be holy to be very evil.[9]

Exciting reading, is it not? What do you make of it? I am pretty well prepared to let it stand as it is. It looks a lot like the story about a religious quack who created some problems in the church. Perhaps we should just let go of the passage and allow it to sink back into oblivion. I would like to do that, but there are several considerations which make me hesitate.

First, Firmilian does not seem to be using a written source. There are no names or other precise details in the account. Second, there is a time lag of over twenty years between when the woman appeared and when Firmilian wrote to Cyprian about her. Third, Firmilian was a man very capable of character assassination when he thought the situation required it. In this same letter he gives his views on heretical baptism, and he attacks Bishop Stephen of Rome (A.D. 254-257), who disagreed with him. In his attack, he bluntly compares Stephen with Judas, the betrayer, charges him with having boasted about his position as bishop of Rome, states that he is worse than the heretics, stresses the harm that he thinks the Roman bishop has done, heaps biting sarcasm onto him, and claims that he has a slippery, shifting, uncertain mind!! If that is how he handles a brother bishop, what would he do with someone he was really mad at?

Fourth, the woman had done plenty to arouse Firmilian's anger. For one thing, she had led away some clergymen. In addition to that, a little later in the letter, Firmilian says that she had also both baptized people and led in the celebrations of the Lord's Supper.

He would have thought this was highly irregular because of her sex.

Keeping all of these considerations before us, maybe, just maybe, what actually went on was quite different from Firmilian's account. Perhaps around A.D. 230-235 a woman who prophesied in ecstasy and who claimed to be inspired by the Holy Spirit did appear in Cappadocia. Maybe she did some rather strange things, but was able to gain a following by virtue of some miracles which she performed. It is possible that her prophecy was in fact legitimate manifestations of the gift of prophecy. The Church, seeing some of its leaders go over to her, may have felt threatened and may have retaliated through an exorcist.

On the other hand, maybe what Firmilian said is 100 percent true, and this material should not be used as evidence that prophecy was still around in Cappadocia in the second quarter of the third century.

I feel skeptical about the material, but I wanted to present it, because it is just possible that Firmilian has given us a distorted picture.

When we look back over the material which Origen and his pupils give us, our picture of the gifts of the Spirit in the third century Church is filled in a little more. Generally speaking, the gifts have slipped in importance. They are still to be found among Christians, as the material from Novatian and Cyprian suggests, but they are becoming much less common than they had been earlier. Origen could find only "traces" of them. Furthermore, even where they were known, there is some evidence that they met with skepticism. Cyprian had to acknowledge that some Christians would not accept what he had to say. Finally, let us note that the Western Church seems to have been more familiar with the gifts in the third century than the Greek Church was. Our evidence from Rome and Carthage is fairly solid, but what we find coming from the East is sparse and shaky.

CONCLUSION

During the almost three hundred years through which we have followed the Church, we have seen many changes. It is staggering to watch the little band of fishermen evolve over the centuries until it becomes one of the most dominant features of the Greek and Latin world. The Church grew astonishingly in size, power, and influence.

When we look for explanations for the growth, we have to start with the Galilean Himself. His divine life and resurrection from the dead gave Him His magnetism. But the sending of the Holy Spirit was extremely important, too. He made the truth about Jesus Christ more real to those early Christians than it had ever been before, and He gave them the power to overcome misunderstanding, hate, and persecution. Through His work in the lives of committed men and women, the name of Christ spread like wildfire.

A part of this whole scene were the gifts of the Spirit. Very frequently it seems, God prompted someone to minister to others. At one time it would be a spoken word, at another, a miraculous deed, and at yet another, an act of compassion. These were the charismata, the gifts of the Spirit, moments when the grace of God would break into human affairs in a special way. As far as we can see, the gifts were an essential part of New Testament Christian living.

The question I raised was what happened after the New Testament period? Did the gifts remain? We then set off, following the gifts through the sources that we have available to us when we study the Early Church.

We have been able to come to a fairly clear conclusion, I think. Throughout the first and second centuries, the gifts remained very important to the Church. We have looked at material from all parts of this period, and we have drawn from virtually every kind of person in the Church. We have heard from bishops and heretics, philosophers and poets, storytellers and theologians. Generally speaking, and of course there must have been exceptions at specific places and times, the Church prior to A.D. 200 was charismatic.

However, in the first half of the third century, things change. We still find evidence that Latin-speaking Christians in the West were familiar with the gifts and open to unusual manifestations of God's presence. Nevertheless, we have to admit that even in the West there were Christians who were raising more than one eyebrow over the gifts. In the Greek East, we hear of only "traces" and we see that what people understand the gifts to be has changed. It is clear that the importance granted to spiritual gifts was passing. This impression is heightened when we realize that a much lower proportion of Christian authors talk about the gifts in this period than before A.D. 200. The gifts just did not occupy the place in the life and thinking of the Church that they once had.

These three centuries saw dramatic changes in the Christian Church. In the midst of all this, the gifts of the Spirit vanished. There came a point around A.D. 260 at which they no longer fitted in the highly organized, well-educated, wealthy, socially-powerful Christian communities. The Church did not lose its soul, but it did lose these special moments when God broke into the lives of men and women.

NOTES

INTRODUCTION

[1]See John 14:25; 15:26; 16:12-14; 2 Tim 1:14; Rom 8:9; Gal 4:6; 5:22 and 23; Eph 1:13 and 14, and Rom 8:26, for example.

[2]Acts 13:1 and 15:32.

[3]1 Cor 12:4-7, 11, and Heb 2:4.

[4]This is diametrically opposed to a position assumed by Benjamin B. Warfield, "The Cessation of the Charismata," in *Counterfeit Miracles* (1918; reprint; Carlisle, Pa.: Banner of Truth, 1976), pp. 3-31. It seems to me that Warfield gets into trouble when he overlooks or brushes aside lightly evidence for the presence of the spiritual gifts that comes from the early second century, which produces a gap between the experience of the Church of the New Testament and the third century. Warfield then accounts for what he regards to be the correct data by saying that the gifts of the Spirit were uniquely associated with the twelve Apostles, authenticating their ministry. They, and those to whom they imparted them, manifested these gifts. He then points to a rapid increase of "wonders" among Christians which began in the late second century and early third century, explaining them by reference to the superstitiousness of the Church's Greco-Roman milieu.

While it is true that superstition grew in the Church around and after A.D. 200, in my opinon the evidence does not suggest that valid gifts ended with the apostolic era. The gifts certainly were important then, but they were not limited to that period. 1 Cor 13:8-12 seems to point to the Second Coming of Christ as the time when the necessity of the ministry of the gifts will come to an end. The historical data suggest that the initial flow of the Spirit's ministry survived the Apostles by several generations.

CHAPTER ONE:
FROM THE EMERGING CHURCH

[1]See M. H. Shepherd, "Didache," in *The Interpreter's Dictionary of the Bible,* ed. E. S. Burke (New York: Abingdon, 1962), 1:842, but A. Adam gives the best discussion to the question of where the *Didache* was written: "Erwägungen zur Hernkunft der Didache," *Zeitschrift für Kirchengeschichte* 67 (1957) 1 - 47.

[2]See R. Glover, "The Didache's Quotations and the Synoptic Gospels," *New Testament Studies* 5 (1958 - 1959) 12 - 29; J.-P. Audet, *La Didaché: Instructions des Apôtres* (Études Bibliques) (Paris: J. Gabalda and Co., 1958), pp. 170ff., and John A. T. Robinson, *Redating the New Testament* (London: SCM, 1976), pp. 322-327.

[3]Audet, *La Didaché,* p. 236. My translation.

[4]Did. 11:7, Audet, *La Didaché,* p. 238. My translation.

[5]It should be pointed out that prophecy and ecstasy were not confined to Christian circles during the first three centuries of our era. This sort of thing is spoken of by many non-Christian authors, including Philo, *Who Is the Heir of Divine Things*, 55, trans. F. H. Colson and G. H. Whitaker, Loeb Classical Library, 4 (London: William Heinemann Ltd., 1932), p. 419; Plotinus, *The Enneads,* 6, 7: 34, and 35, trans. S. MacKenna, rev. by B. D. Page, (2d ed., London: Faber and Faber, 1956), pp. 588f.; Cicero, *On Divination,* 1, 66, trans. W. A. Falconer, Loeb Classical Library (London: William Heinemann, 1923), p. 297; Sophocles, *Antigone,* 956-963, trans. F. Storr, Loeb Classical Library, 1 (London: William Heinemann, 1912), p. 387; Euripides, *Bacchae,* 1122ff., ed. E. R. Dodds, (Oxford: Clarendon Press, 1944), p. 65, and Plato, *Phaedrus,* 244B, trans. H. N. Fowler, Loeb Classical Library, 1 (London: William Heinemann, 1914), p. 465. In addition to the comments made by these authors, A. D. Nock, *Conversion* (Oxford: Clarendon Press, 1933), draws attention to two men who seem to have had unusual powers of some sort; Apollonius of Tyana, who lived in the late first century (p. 196) and Alexander of Abunoteichus, who was active ca. A.D. 150 (p. 93).

[6]Audet, *La Didaché,* p. 238. My translation.

[7]*Ibid.*

[8]H. von Campenhausen, *Ecclesiastical Authority and Spiritual Power,* trans. J. A. Baker (London: Adam and Charles Black, 1969), p. 178.

[9]von Campenhausen, p. 295.

[10]Did. 15:1 and 2; Audet, *La Didaché,* p. 240. My translation.

[11]See p. 2 above.

[12]See L. W. Barnard, *Studies in the Apostolic Fathers and Their Background* (Oxford: Basil Blackwell, 1966), p. 12 and Robinson, *Redating the New Testament,* pp. 330ff.

[13]*1 Clement* 38:1; Holt H. Graham, trans., (The Apostolic Fathers: A New Translation and Commentary, ed. R. M. Grant, 2) (New York: Nelson, 1965), p. 66.

CHAPTER TWO: FROM THE SHADOWS

[1]Johannes Quasten, *Patrology* (Utrecht-Antwerp: Spectrum Publishers, 1966), 1: 63.

[2]Ignatius, "Polycarp," 2:2, *Ignace d'Antioch: Lettres,* ed. P. Th. Camelot (Sources chrétiennes, 10) (4th. ed., Paris: Cerf, 1969), p. 148. My translation.

[3]Ignatius, "To the Philadelphians," 7:1 and 2, ed. Camelot, *Ignace d'Antioch: Lettres,* p. 126. My translation.

[4]*The Mysticism of Ignatius of Antioch* (Ph.D. Thesis, The University of Pennsylvania, 1932), p. 50.

[5]See the studies of G. F. Snyder, *The Shepherd of Hermas,* The Apostolic Fathers: A New Translation and Commentary, ed. R. M. Grant, 6 (Camden, N.J.: Thomas Nelson and Sons, 1968), pp. 22ff.; S. Giet, *Hermas et les Pasteurs: les trois auteurs de Pasteur d'Hermas* (Paris: Presses Universitaires de France, 1963), pp. 304f., and Robinson, *Redating the New Testament,* pp. 319ff.

[6]1:3ff.; 5:1ff.; 8:1ff.; 9:6ff.; 18:7ff.; 22:6ff.; 25:2ff. I am following a method of dividing the text of *The Shepherd* which was suggested by R. A. B. Mynors and which presents a continuous numbering of the chapters as an alternative to the traditional division into Visions, Mandates, and Similitudes.

[7]*The Shepherd of Hermas,* 43:7 and 16, trans. Snyder, pp. 87 and 88.

[8]H. B. Swete, *The Holy Spirit in the Ancient Church* (London: MacMillan, 1912), p. 25.

[9]See also Kirsopp Lake, "The Shepherd of Hermas and Christian Life in the Second Century," *Harvard Theological Review* 4 (1911) 45.

[10]Trans. Snyder, *The Shepherd of Hermas,* pp. 87f.

CHAPTER THREE: FROM SPIRIT AND MIND

[1] For those who wish to pursue these matters further, J. H. Charlesworth's article "The Odes of Solomon—Not Gnostic," *Catholic Biblical Quarterly* 31 (1969) 357-369 would be a good place to start. After that, there is a great deal of material available.

[2] R. M. Grant, "The Odes of Solomon and the Church of Antioch," *Journal of Biblical Literature* 63 (1944) 368.

[3] This and all the following quotations of *The Odes* are from the J. R. Harris and A. Mingana translation: *The Odes and Psalms of Solomon,* (2d. ed., Manchester: At the University Press, 1920), vol. 2.

[4] Harris and Mingana, *The Odes and Psalms of Solomon,* 2: 297f.

[5] Alexander Roberts and James Donaldson, trans., *The Ante-Nicene Fathers,* ed. Alexander Roberts, James Donaldson, and A. C. Coxe, (2d. ed., Buffalo: Christian Literature Publishing Company, 1885), 1: 214.

[6] *Dialogue,* 39 and 1 Cor 12:9.

[7] *Dialogue,* 39 and Rom 12:7.

[8] *Dialogue,* 82: Roberts and Donaldson, *The Ante-Nicene Fathers,* 1: 240.

[9] *Ibid.*

[10] *Dialogue,* 87: Roberts and Donaldson, *The Ante-Nicene Fathers,* 1: 243.

[11] See L. W. Barnard, "Justin Martyr in Recent Study," *Scottish Journal of Theology* 22 (1969) 152; *Justin Martyr: His Life and Thought* (Cambridge: At the University Press, 1967), p. 134, by the same author; Henry Chadwick, *The Early Church,* (The Pelican History of the Church, 1 Penguin Books, 1967), pp. 48 and 261f.; Hans Lietzmann, *The Founding of the Church Universal,* (A History of the Early Church, trans. B. L. Woolf, 2; London: Lutterworth Press, 1961), p. 125f.; J. N. D. Kelly, *Early Christian Doctrines* (4th ed., London: Adam and Charles Black, 1968), pp. 89ff. and 194ff.: and *Early Christian Creeds,* (2d. ed., London: Longmans, 1960), pp. 43 and 70ff., by the same author.

[12] See p. 17f. above.

[13] See pp. 24 - 27 above.

[14] G. T. Purves, *The Testimony of Justin Martyr to Early Christianity* (London: James Nisbet & Co., n.d.), p. 45. This is supported by material in Barnard's book, *Justin Martyr: His Life and Thought,* pp. 133 and 150.

CHAPTER FOUR: FROM THE CHURCH FRINGE

[1]See Eusebius' *Chronicle*, Bk. 2, under the 173d. year of Christ, (Migne, *Patrologia Graeca,* 19), col. 563; his *Ecclesiastical History,* 5, preface, 1, trans. Kirsopp Lake, Loeb Classical Library (London: William Heinemann, 1926), 1: 405; also 5, 3:4; 1: 443, and 4, 27:1; 1: 393f., and Epiphanius, *Panarion,* 48:1, (Migne, *Patrologia Graeca,* 41), col. 856. Pierre de Labriolle, who produced the most adequate study yet done on Montanism, accepts this date (*La crise montaniste* [Paris: Ernest Leroux, 1913], p. 573), as do W. H. C. Frend, *The Early Church,* [Knowing Christianity] (London: Hodder and Stoughton, 1965), p. 80 and T. D. Barnes, "Chronology of Montanism," *Journal of Theological Studies,* n.s., 21 (Oct. 1970) 403 - 408—one of the few points on which these last two scholars agree.

[2]For a rather favorable reaction to Montanism, see John de Soyres, *Montanism and the Primitive Church* (Cambridge: Deighton, Bell and Co., 1878), p. 110, which stands in marked contrast to an impassioned portrayal in Henri Daniel-Rops' *The Church of Apostles and Martyrs,* trans. A. Butler, (History of the Church of Christ, 1) (London: J. M. Dent & Sons Ltd., 1960), p. 297.

[3]*Panarion,* 48:4 (Migne, *Patrologia Graeca,* 41), col. 861. My translation.

[4]Didymus, *On the Trinity,* 3:41, (Migne, *Patrologia Graeca,* 39), col. 984. My translation.

[5]Epiphanius, *Panarion,* 48:12; col. 873. My translation.

[6]Justin, *I Apology,* 31 and 44, and *Dialogue with Trypho,* 37, trans. Alexander Roberts and James Donaldson, (*The Ante-Nicene Fathers,* 1) (Buffalo: Christian Literature Publishing Company, 1885), pp. 173, 177, and 213.

[7]Theophilus, *To Autolycus,* 3, 7, trans. Marcus Dods, (*Ante-Nicene Fathers,* 2), p. 116.

[8]Athenagoras, *A Plea for the Christians,* 9, trans. B. P. Pratten, (*Ante-Nicene Fathers,* 2), p. 133.

[9]See pp. 20 - 24 above.

[10]See p. 31f. above.

[11]Eusebius, *Ecclesiastical History,* 5, 16:17, Lake, (Loeb Classical Library), 1: 481.

[12]Eusebius, *Ecclesiastical History,* 5, 16:7, Lake, (Loeb Classical Library), 1: 475.

¹³Eusebius, *Ecclesiastical History,* 5, 16:9, Lake, (Loeb Classical Library), 1: 477.

¹⁴Eusebius, *Ecclesiastical History,* 5, 16:12, Lake, (Loeb Classical Library), 1: 479.

¹⁵*The Church History of Eusebius,* trans. A. C. McGiffert, (Nicene and Post-Nicene Fathers, series 2, 1) (Grand Rapids: Eerdmans, 1951), p. 232.

¹⁶*The Ecclesiastical History and the Martyrs of Palestine,* trans. J. E. L. Oulton (London: S. P. C. K., 1954), p. 160.

¹⁷G. W. H. Lampe, *A Patristic Greek Lexicon* (Oxford: At the Clarendon Press, 1961), p. 88.

¹⁸K. S. Latourette, *A History of Christianity* (New York: Harper & Row, 1953), p. 128 and Emile Lombard, "Le montanisme et l'inspiration," *Revue de Théologie et de Philosophie,* n.s., 3 (1915) 299 arrived at the same conclusion independently. Others, among them Pierre de Labriolle (p. 171), also acknowledge the signs of tongue speaking to be seen among the Montanists.

¹⁹P. Koetschau, ed., *Die griechischen christlichen Schriftsteller,* 4 (Leipzig: J. C. Hindrich, 1899), p. 160. My translation.

²⁰Origen, *Against Celsus,* 7, 2, trans. Henry Chadwick (Cambridge: University Press, 1953), p. 395.

²¹*Against Celsus,* 7, 3, Chadwick, pp. 395f.

²²*Against Celsus,* 7, 3, Chadwick, p. 396.

²³*Against Celsus,* 7, 10, Chadwick, p. 403.

²⁴*The Founding of the Church Universal,* A History of the Early Church, trans. B. L. Woolf, 2, (London: Lutterworth Press, 1961), p. 55. H. Weinel, in an early study of the gifts of the Spirit, says the same thing, *Die Wirkungen des Geistes und der Geister im nachapostolischen Zeitalter bis auf Irenäus* (Freiburg: J. C. B. Mohr [Paul Siebeck], 1899), p. 76.

²⁵*Against Celsus,* 7, 8, Chadwick, p. 401.

CHAPTER FIVE: FROM BISHOPS

¹For an introduction to Gnosticism, see R. McL. Wilson's *The Gnostic Problem* (London: A. R. Mowbray and Co., 1958).

²R. McL. Wilson, *Gnosis and the New Testament* (Philadelphia: Fortress Press, 1968), p. 16. See also G. van Groningen, *First Century Gnosticism: Its Origins and Motifs* (Leiden: E. J. Brill, 1967), pp. 4, 129, n. 5, and 173.

³This is Irenaeus as quoted by Eusebius in his *Ecclesiastical*

History, 5, 7:3 - 5, Kirsopp Lake, (Loeb Classical Library), 1:453 and 455. The Greek text was chosen here and in the next quotation because of the relative weakness of the Latin text which was edited by W. W. Harvey (1852).

There are also four other passages from *Against Heresies* which may shed some light upon what Irenaeus knew about the gifts of the Spirit. The first is 4, 7:3, where Irenaeus speaks of prophecy in a way which suggests that it still may have been a present phenomenon. The second passage is 4, 53:2, which compares three gifts that were still active: love, knowledge, and prophecy. The third passage, 4, 52:3, is where Irenaeus speaks as though he is giving a warning to false prophets who are still alive and menacing the Church. The last is 3, 11:12. In this selection, Irenaeus is speaking of prophecy as if he personally approved of it. While all of these passages may be interpreted as giving proof of the continuation of the gifts of the Spirit, none is strong enough to have much weight placed on it.

[4]"The Cessation of the Charismata," p. 15 and pp. 241f., n. 31.

[5]Irenaeus as quoted by Eusebius in *Ecclesiastical History*, 5, 7:6, Kirsopp Lake, (Loeb Classical Library), 1: 455.

[6]See *Ecclesiastical History*, 5, 7:1 and 6, Kirsopp Lake, (Loeb Classical Library), 1: 451 and 455.

[7]For detailed evaluations of Eusebius' work as an historian, see H. J. Lawlor, *Eusebius* (1928; reprint, London: S. P. C. K., 1954); J. Stevenson, *Studies in Eusebius* (Cambridge: W. Heffer & Sons Ltd., 1933), D. S. Wallace-Hadrill, *Eusebius of Caesarea* (Westminster, Maryland: Canterbury Press, 1961), and R. M. Grant, *Eusebius as Church Historian* (Oxford: Clarendon Press, 1980).

[8]1:442, Loeb Classical Library (London: William Heinemann, 1926). My translation.

[9]*Orthodoxy and Heresy in Earliest Christianity*, trans. and ed. R. A. Kraft and G. Krodel (Philadelphia: Fortress Press, 1971), p. 191.

CHAPTER SIX:
FROM HERESY AND SUPERSTITION

[1]Clement of Alexandria, *Excerpta ex Theodoto*, 24:1, ed. R. P. Casey (London: Christophers, 1934), p. 58.

[2]*La Gnose Valentinienne* (Paris: Librairie Philosophique J. Vrin, 1947), pp. 302f.

[3]*An Introduction to the Apocrypha* (New York: Oxford

University Press, 1957), p. 263.

⁴"Acts of Peter," 2, trans. G. C. Stead, E. Hennecke, *New Testament Apocrypha*, ed. W. Schneemelcher, trans. and ed. R. McL. Wilson (London: Lutterworth Press, 1965), 2: 280.

⁵"Acts of Paul," 11, 1, trans. R. McL. Wilson, *New Testament Apocrypha*, 2: 383.

⁶"Acts of John," 46, trans. G. C. Stead, *New Testament Apocrypha*, 2: 238.

⁷"Acts of John," 56; Stead, *New Testament Apocrypha*, 2: 242.

⁸"Acts of Paul," 9; Wilson, *New Testament Apocrypha*, 2: 379.

⁹*Ibid.*

¹⁰"Acts of Paul," 11, 3; Wilson, *New Testament Apocrypha*, 2: 385.

¹¹"Acts of Paul," 9; Wilson, *New Testament Apocrypha*, 2: 379f.

¹²"The Beginning of the Stay in Ephesus," trans. R. McL. Wilson, *New Testament Apocrypha*, 2: 387f.

¹³"Acts of Peter," 4, 11; Wilson, *New Testament Apocrypha*, 2: 293.

¹⁴"Acts of Andrew," trans. Ernest Best, *New Testament Apocrypha*, 2; 407. Other passages presenting similar experiences are: "Acts of Paul," 6; 2: 369; "Acts of Thomas," 41, trans. R. McL. Wilson, *New Testament Apocrypha*, 2: 267f., and "Acts of Thomas," 68; 2: 483f.

¹⁵Irenaeus, *Against Heresies*, 2, 49:3. See p. 50 above.

¹⁶"Acts of Paul," 4; 2: 365. See "Acts of Peter," 9; 2: 314; "Acts of Thomas," 53 and 54; 2: 472f.; "Acts of John," 23; 2: 218f.; 37; 2: 224, and "Acts of Paul," 11, 1; 2: 383f. for records of similar events.

¹⁷"Acts of Peter," 26 and 27; 2: 309; "Acts of Paul," 8; 2: 378; "Acts of Thomas," 33; 2: 461; 54; 2: 473, and 81; 2: 486; "Acts of John," 24; 2: 219; 47; 2: 239; 52; 2: 240; 75; 2: 249; 80; 2: 251, and 83; 2: 252.

CHAPTER SEVEN: FROM ROME

¹James L. Ash, Jr. argues that the prophet and the bishop represented conflicting forms of government in the Early Church and that the former disappeared when his functions were taken over by the latter ("The Decline of Ecstatic Prophecy," *Theological Studies* 37 [1976] 227-252). The decline of the

charismata followed the appearance of bishops, but one cannot, therefore, assume a cause and effect relationship. The evidence suggests that none of the charismata ever became the exclusive preserve of bishops. See pp. 28ff.; 31ff.; 42ff.; 48ff.; 53ff. above and 64ff.; 67ff.; 73ff.; 77ff., and 83ff. below. The disappearance of the gifts should be understood as one part of the process of sophistication which the Church experienced.

²See his *Refutation of all Heresies,* 9, 6 and 7, trans. J. H. MacMahon, (*The Ante-Nicene Fathers,* ed. Alexander Roberts, James Donaldson, and A. C. Coxe, 5) (Buffalo: The Christian Literature Company, 1886), p. 128ff.

³*The Treatise on the Apostolic Tradition of St. Hippolytus of Rome* (London: S. P. C. K., 1937), p. xliv.

⁴John E. Stam, "Charismatic Theology in the *Apostolic Tradition* of Hippolytus," in *Current Issues in Biblical and Patristic Interpretation* (Grand Rapids: Eerdmans, 1975), pp. 267-276.

⁵Hippolytus, *The Apostolic Tradition,* 15:1, trans. Gregory Dix (London: S. P. C. K., 1937), p. 22.

⁶Hippolytus, *Apostolic Tradition,* 35:3, trans. Dix; p. 54.

⁷B. S. Easton came to a similar conclusion. See his *The Apostolic Tradition of Hippolytus* (Cambridge: At the University Press, 1934), p. 104.

⁸Dix, trans., *The Apostolic Tradition,* p. 62.

⁹Novatian, *Concerning the Trinity,* 29, 10, (Corpus Christianorum, ed. G. F. Diercks, Series Latina, 4) (Turnholt: Brepols, 1972), p. 70. My translation.

¹⁰Novatian, *Concerning the Trinity,* 29, 4, (Corpus Christianorum, 4), p. 69. My translation.

¹¹See Russell J. DeSimone, *The Treatise of Novatian, the Roman Presbyter on the Trinity,* (Studia Ephemeridis Augustinianum, 4) (Rome: Institutum patristicum Augustinianum, 1970), pp. 143; 147f., and 158.

¹²Novatian, *Concerning the Trinity,* 29, 16, (Corpus Christianorum, 4), p. 71. My translation.

¹³ Novatian, *Concerning the Trinity,* 29, 18 and 19, (Corpus Christianorum, 4), p. 71. My translation.

¹⁴Novatian, *Concerning the Trinity,* 29, 19, (Corpus Christianorum, 4), p. 71. My translation.

¹⁵*Ibid.*

¹⁶Novatian, *Concerning the Trinity,* 29, 26, (Corpus Christianorum, 4), p. 72. My translation.

CHAPTER EIGHT: FROM CARTHAGE

[1]See T. D. Barnes, *Tertullian* (Oxford: Clarendon Press, 1971), pp. 10ff.

[2]I do not think this question has been adequately handled by anyone yet, but useful contributions to the discussion may be found in H. J. Lawlor, "The Heresy of the Phrygians," *Eusebiana* (Oxford: Clarendon Press, 1912), pp. 108 - 135; R. G. Smith, "Tertullian and Montanism," *Theology* 46 (1943) 127 - 136, and Pierre de Labriolle, *La crise montaniste* (Paris: Ernest Leroux, 1913), *passim.* Douglas Powell's treatment of the question in "Tertullianists and Cataphrygians," *Vigiliae Christianae* 29, 1 (1975) 33-54 is particularly helpful.

[3]Tertullian, *Adversus Marcionem* (*Against Marcion*), ed. and trans. Ernest Evans (Oxford: Clarendon Press, 1972), 2: 561.

[4]Tertullian, *De Anima* (*Concerning the Soul*), 9, 4, ed. J. H. Waszink, Corpus Christianorum, Series Latina 2, part 2) (Turnholt: Brepols, 1954), 792f.

[5]Tertullian, *De Anima,* 9, 3, (Corpus Christianorum, 2, part 2), p. 792. My translation.

[6]Tertullian, *De Anima,* 9, 4, (Corpus Christianorum, 2, part 2), p. 793.

[7]Tertullian, *De Monogamie* (*Concerning Monogamy*), 1, 2, ed. E. Dekkers, (Corpus Christianorum, Series Latina, 2, part 2) (Turnholt: Brepols, 1954), p. 1229. My translation.

[8]See the discussion of this in Johannes Quasten's *Patrology* (Utrecht-Antwerp: Spectrum, 1966), 1: 181.

[9]Tertullian, *Passio S. Perpetuae* (*Martyrdom of St. Perpetuae*), 1, ed. J. A. Robinson, (Texts and Studies 1, 2 Cambridge, 1891), p. 62. My translation.

[10]J. G. Ph. Borleffs. ed., (Corpus Christianorum, Series Latina, 1, part 2) (Turnholt: Brepols, 1954), p. 295. My translation.

[11]See G. S. M. Walker, *The Churchmanship of St. Cyprian,* (Ecumenical Studies in History, 9) (London: Lutterworth Press, 1968), p. 10 and H. von Campenhausen, *The Fathers of the Latin Church,* trans. H. Hoffman (London: Adam & Charles Black, 1964), p. 46.

[12]A. von Harnack, "Cyprian als Enthusiast (Cyprian as an Enthusiast)," *Zeitschrift für neutestamentliche Wissenschaft* 3 (1902) 177 - 191.

[13]*Epistulae Cypriani* (*Letters of Cyprian*), 78, 2, ed. G. Hartel, (Corpus Scriptorum Ecclesiasticorum Latinorum, 3, 2) (Vindobon: C. Geroldi, 1871), p. 837. My translation.

[14]Harnack, "Cyprian als Enthusiast," p. 188.

[15]Cyprian, *Epistulae*, 66, 10, (Corpus Scriptorum, 3, 2), p. 734. My translation.

[16]Cyprian, *De mortalitate* (*Concerning Mortality*), 19, ed. G. Hartel, (Corpus Scriptorum Ecclesiasticorum Latinorum, 3, 1) (Vindobon: C. Geroldi, 1868), p. 309. My translation.

[17]*Ibid.*

[18]Cyprian, *Epistulae*, 16, 4, (Corpus Scriptorum, 3, 2), p. 520. My translation.

CHAPTER NINE: FROM THE GREEK EAST

[1]Jean Daniélou, *Origen,* trans. W. Mitchell (London and New York: Sheed and Ward, 1955), p. 27.

[2]Origen, *Against Celsus,* 1, 2, trans. Henry Chadwick (Cambridge: At the University Press), p. 8.

[3]Origen, *Against Celsus,* 1, 46, Chadwick, p. 42.

[4]Origen, *Against Celsus,* 2, 8, Chadwick, p. 72.

[5]Origen, *Against Celsus,* 7, 8, Chadwick, pp. 401f.

[6]Daniélou, *Origen,* p. 27.

[7]Dionysius in Eusebius' *Ecclesiastical History,* 6, 40:3, trans. J. E. L. Oulton (London: William Heinemann, 1964), 2: 97.

[8]Dionysius in Eusebius, *Ecclesiastical History,* 7, 7:3; Oulton, 2: 143 and 145.

[9]Firmilian, *Epistulae Cypriani,* 75, 10, ed. G. Hartel, (Corpus Scriptorum Ecclesiasticorum Latinorum, 3, 2) (Vindobon: C. Geroldi, 1871), pp. 816ff. My translation.

Index